Functional Awareness

T0355077

Functional Awareness

Anatomy in Action for Dancers

Second Edition

Nancy Romita and Allegra Romita

OXFORD
UNIVERSITY PRESS

OXFORD
UNIVERSITY PRESS

Oxford University Press is a department of the University of Oxford. It furthers
the University's objective of excellence in research, scholarship, and education
by publishing worldwide. Oxford is a registered trade mark of Oxford University
Press in the UK and certain other countries.

Published in the United States of America by Oxford University Press
198 Madison Avenue, New York, NY 10016, United States of America.

© Oxford University Press 2023

Library of Congress Cataloging-in-Publication Data
Names: Romita, Nancy, author. | Romita, Allegra, author.
Title: Functional awareness : anatomy in action for dancers /
Nancy Romita, Allegra Romita.
Description: Second edition. | New York, NY : Oxford University Press, [2023] |
Includes bibliographical references and index. |
Contents: The relationship of habit to dance training—Dynamic alignment and the 4Rs—
Impact of thinking on doing—Motions of the trunk and use of spiral—
Core support—The pelvis and hip joint—The knee—The ankle and foot—
Walking and weight shift—Expressivity of arms—Breath—Restore toward balance
Identifiers: LCCN 2022060604 (print) | LCCN 2022060605 (ebook) |
ISBN 9780197586815 (hardback) | ISBN 9780197586822 (paperback) |
ISBN 9780197586846 (epub) | ISBN 9780197586853
Subjects: LCSH: Dance—Physiological aspects. | Dancers—Training of. |
Mind and body. | Muscular sense.
Classification: LCC RC1220.D35 R66 2023 (print) | LCC RC1220.D35 (ebook)
| DDC 617.1/0275—dc23/eng/20221219
LC record available at https://lccn.loc.gov/2022060604
LC ebook record available at https://lccn.loc.gov/2022060605

DOI: 10.1093/oso/9780197586815.001.0001

Paperback printed by Marquis Book Printing, Canada
Hardback printed by Bridgeport National Bindery, Inc., United States of America

Contents

Acknowledgments

The authors thank the many people who supported this project by the generous gift of their time and talents. The authors owe a supreme debt of gratitude to Norm Hirschy of Oxford University Press whose encouragement and belief in our work sustains our courage to move thoughts from the dance studio and teaching classroom to the written page.

Many thanks to Jim Burger for his artistic talents and photographs, Hollis McCracken for her pencil drawing, and Mary Hamlin Spencer and William Spencer for their feedback after reading through the manuscript while it was in its developmental processes. Additionally, we would like to thank Caitlin Hughes for her beautiful anatomical images throughout the book.

We honor the memory of Betsy Winship, our friend and guide to editing and book publishing during our first and second books. Her encouragement, keen eye, and her presence are missed.

Finally, both authors express deep gratitude to Vic Romita, loving husband and father, for his continued enthusiasm and support for all our artistic endeavors.

Introduction

The second edition of *Functional Awareness: Anatomy in Action for Dancers* provides practical information about how the body functions and how this information can improve dance skills. This book is a guide to self-care, injury prevention, and dancer wellness through embodied explorations and anatomical visualizations. A primary precept of Functional Awareness® (FA) is honoring individual differences in skeletal structure and learning modalities.

This second edition contains new findings, new research, and new somatic explorations to improve dance performance and enriches the first edition in several ways. It seeks to support a broader spectrum of dance forms, and it invites the reader to investigate new strategies to enhance understanding of movement function and discover efficacy in action. The authors emphasize that Functional Awareness practices support the aesthetics of all dance forms. Thus, this second edition incorporates examples from many dance styles and movement practices.

Our research investigates a variety of cueing strategies to help support student learning of movement function as well as ways to show how Functional Awareness can be useful in both the dance classroom and in daily life. The strategies include anatomical visualizations, tactile experiences, visual cues, and mental training to improve sensory-motor control.

Many dance forms have a tradition in which dancers of one generation glean movement knowledge from their mentors, then use that knowledge to create variations and new dance forms. Functional Awareness is an approach to embodied anatomy with roots in the somatic wisdom of our antecedents. The authors' work rests on a foundation of deep practices in several somatic and scientific fields along with experience in professional dance performance, choreography, and dance education. We honor the wisdom and knowledge that has led us to this point, as well as our artistic and somatic mentors all of which profoundly inform the Functional Awareness lens on human movement potential.

As co-authors, we bring distinctive experiences to this collaborative effort. Allegra (MA, EdM, CMA, RYT) currently works in the Dance Education program at the Steinhardt School of Culture, Education, and Human Development at New York University. She graduated from the University of Michigan with a BFA in Dance and a minor in Movement Science and received both an MA in Dance Education from NYU Steinhardt and an EdM in Motor Learning & Control from Teachers College, Columbia University. Allegra is Artistic Visioning Partner of New York City–based dance-theater collective Sydnie L. Mosley Dances. Allegra is a Certified Movement Analyst in Laban Movement Analysis (LMA) through the

Functional Awareness. Second Edition. Nancy Romita and Allegra Romita, Oxford University Press.
© Oxford University Press 2023. DOI: 10.1093/oso/9780197586815.003.0001

Laban/Bartenieff Institute of Movement Studies. She is also a certified yoga teacher and teaches yoga at Brooklyn Yoga Project and Heatwise in Brooklyn, New York. Nancy (MFA, AmSAT, RSME) is Senior Lecturer at Towson University and director of Alexander Technique MidAtlantic Teacher Training. She was Artistic Director of The Moving Company from 1993 to 2001. She has 40 years of experience teaching dance, anatomy, and somatic movement practices. Our varied dance trainings and somatic backgrounds were combined to form a connected process that stands as its own somatic approach.

In the seven years since the first edition of this book was published, Functional Awareness has developed and deepened as an approach to embodied anatomy through reflective practice. We wish to acknowledge the collective wisdom of the dance educators in each Functional Awareness® Movement Educator Certification cohort for their efforts in integrating the FA philosophy and practices into a multitude of dance forms for differing student populations. We are grateful for our anatomy mentors, dance teachers, somatics guides, and the contemporary research of peers for the profound influences on the information disseminated in this book.

This book is written for all dance enthusiasts interested in learning more about the body. The book is for dancers, movement educators, professional dancers, and somatic practitioners. It is not an anatomy text but rather a book introducing some anatomical concepts to provide cognitive context for sensory explorations. It includes basic principles of anatomy to enhance understanding of how the body can move with less stress and greater ease. The movement explorations and anatomical information establish a platform for ongoing exploration, discovery, and discussion. The material aggregates so as to create building blocks for mindful patterns in daily movement. Traveling through the book, the reader learns to honor and understand individual differences in the human structure and how to discover greater movement potential within their own body.

The format for the book is as follows:

Each chapter
- o Includes a story to draw the reader into the chapter material and to provide context for learning the functional movement and anatomy information.
- o Provides movement explorations and anatomical visualizations to enhance and deepen understanding of movement function.
- o Suggests strategies to apply during dance training and performance.
- o Invites practices in daily life to help repattern unconscious habitual movements that compromise efficiency in action and are often a source of chronic discomfort and pain.

In addition to introducing essential concepts in functional anatomy, the book examines daily posture and movement habits. This book proposes the notion that physical training (in the gym, on the mat, or in the studio) can be compromised by small unconscious movement habits and patterns that have the potential to negate the hard work achieved during dance training and cross training. Understanding movement habits and their inadvertent consequences can enable each dancer to change unwanted and unnecessary movement patterns and develop new ways of moving. Consistent mindful practice of body awareness during quotidian tasks can potentially result in recuperation from the rigorous requirements of moving through life.

Functional Awareness invites a lively curiosity into body understanding. It is a practice of assessment through non-judgment. FA honors varied dance trainings and aesthetics. All bodies have the potential for artistic expressivity within the dancer's individual structure. In dance, we constantly seek the end-ranges of movement and often achieve spectacular artistic results. At times, this results in a cost to our physical structure. Applied practice of the Functional Awareness principles enables one to efficiently recruit muscle actions to improve dance technique, release unnecessary muscular tension, and develop a balance between exertion and recuperation. The movement explorations within the book are not prescriptive; rather, they enhance body knowledge and develop self-agency in movement practice and in daily life. The book provides methods, rooted in embodied anatomy, to empower one's unique body/mind structure toward full artistic expression within any dance aesthetic. It is our quest to develop strategies for stability and recovery and to provide accessible tools so people can move for a lifetime with ease and grace.

We invite the reader to apply each chapter's concepts to dance skills as well as more broadly during everyday tasks. Discovering daily mindfulness of body choices develops a profound deepening of one's dance artistry, while providing recuperation from the end-range actions of the rigorous requirements of dance. Each chapter of this book allows the reader to investigate the Functional Awareness values of acceptance, discovery learning, assessment with non-judgment, and self-advocacy in dance.

1

The Relationship of Habit to Dance Training

Functional Awareness (FA) is a practice in embodied anatomy to deepen understanding of movement function, improve dynamic alignment, and enhance expressivity and artistry required in any form of dance. This book is an anatomical guide to self-care and injury prevention for dancers and draws on the somatic processes of Functional Awareness. The approach investigates information about the skeletal structure, the muscle structure, and the myofascial tissue to help sustain elasticity, flexibility, and efficiency in movement. In addition, the FA approach focuses on developing awareness and applications outside the dance training classroom to encourage practices for dancer wellness during activities of daily life.

People often experience tension or pain and assume this is something that "just happens" to them. It is as if the body is a separate entity. We may think of joint and body pain as being similar to a cold virus that we just pick up from somewhere. There might be a particular event that precipitates the pain, but often it is not one specific action that leads to the discomfort. Most muscular discomfort arises from unconscious repeated movement habits. If the action is repeated with frequency, it creates wear on the system and leads to pain and discomfort over time. In a sense, people "practice" discomfort through unconscious posture and daily movement choices. The following is an old joke to illustrate this point.

The Story: How Your Suit Fits

A woman has taken her pantsuit to be fixed and altered by a tailor. She tries on the outfit to be sure the alterations are correct. As she tries on the pants, she notices the leg lengths appear different. The tailor is not interested in doing more work so he just adjusts her hip a bit and now the legs look even. The woman adjusts and decides she can live with this. The woman now tries on the jacket and discovers one sleeve is too long and the darts make the jacket hard to button in the front. The tailor says, "Look, if you just make this little adjustment in your shoulders, it will fit perfectly." The woman buys into this sales pitch, makes the adjustment, and walks out of the store. As she is walking out of the store and down the street, two people are coming at her from the opposite direction. One person comments on the contorted figure walking

Functional Awareness. Second Edition. Nancy Romita and Allegra Romita, Oxford University Press.
© Oxford University Press 2023. DOI: 10.1093/oso/9780197586815.003.0002

toward then and says, "Look at that poor woman." "Yes," the other one replies, "but doesn't her suit fit perfectly!"

This old joke illustrates subtle and obvious adjustments we make in life. These adjustments become patterns that are unconscious. Over time the patterns begin to take a physical toll on our system. This toll is exhibited as tension, pain, stiffness, or rigidity of movement. The good news: It is possible to shift posture and movement habits and discover more ease and less tension in the body. Here are three simple approaches:

1. Become aware of your personal movement habits.
2. Learn a basic understanding of how the musculoskeletal system functions and how this affects body action.
3. Practice mindfulness in action to improve movement function and dynamic alignment.

Exploration: Become Aware of Movement Habits

1. Clasp your hands together with all your fingers crossed.
2. Notice which thumb is on top. Is it your dominant (writing) hand or your non-dominant hand?
3. Open your hands and close them quickly and unconsciously. Do your thumbs and hands have the same arrangement again?
4. Now release your hands and reweave you fingers to make the other thumb end up on top. How familiar or unfamiliar is this? Does it take a little more time for your brain to tell your body to place your hands in this way?

Try the same activity with your arms crossed.

1. Fold your arms.
2. Notice which arm is on the top. Is this the same arm as the thumb earlier?
3. Drop your arms by your side and now fold the arms with the opposite forearm on top. How does this feel?

Try the same activity with legs crossed.

1. Cross your legs, or your ankles if that is more familiar to you.
2. Notice which leg is on the top. Is this the same leg as the arm earlier?
3. Uncross the legs and then try the other side. How does this feel?

Often, we do have a preferred way we clasp our hands or fold our arms and the other position can feel a bit peculiar. In facilitating this activity for over 40 years with thousands of people, we realize that these habits are not systemic and have no pattern regarding dominant hand or genetic proclivity. They are merely "how your suit fits" or how you have made a habitual accommodation over time. Some habits are compulsory and very positive, such as brushing our teeth or automatically moving the foot to the brake pad when a light turns yellow and then red. Some habits are unnecessary. Unconscious habits with posture can compromise body balance, place unnecessary stress on the system, and lead to discomfort and pain. Improving your range of choices for movement develops a more resilient neuromuscular system.

Your Findings and Why They Matter

Almost two-thirds of all injuries in dance are related to mis-stacking or misalignment of bony structures (Leiderbach, 2018). Sometimes a subtle habit, such as constantly sitting with weight more into one hip, causes mis-stacking and becomes a factor leading to potential injury. Frequent unconscious misuse of the body can lead to chronic discomfort or pain. Folding your hands does not have a significant impact on your neuromuscular system, but crossing your arms often leads to many other accommodations to the spine and can develop patterns of imbalance. Crossing one specific leg may lead to an imbalance in the hips. If your legs are crossed right now, notice whether you have more weight on one hip. This creates instability in the lumbar spine and pelvis. It can be detrimental to the body, leading to pain or discomfort under the rigors of dance training. Hence, how you move through daily action affects how you dance.

The Anatomy: The Skeletal Structure

Anatomical knowledge is key both to understanding how the body performs and to developing personal agency. This information can help prevent mis-stacking of the skeletal structure and unintended injury. It is useful to be able to identify the bones of our skeletal structure. (See Figure 1.1.) Our skeletal structure is the internal framework that supports the body, helps to define the human shape, and facilitates movement. In addition, the skeletal system produces blood cells and protects internal organs.

Each human body has individual skeletal and muscular differences. Generally, there are 206 bones in the body, yet the number does vary from person to person. For example, 15% to 30% of people have an os trigonum, a floating bone in the foot. There is also variety in how the bones are shaped and this variety can affect movement function.

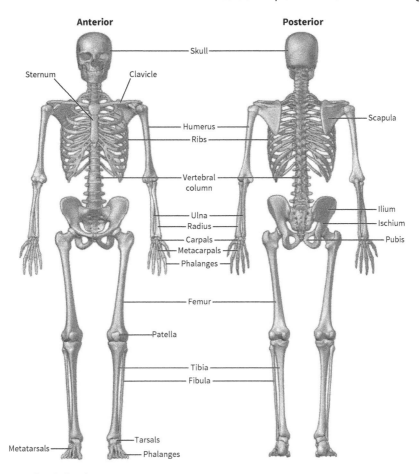

Figure 1.1 The skeletal system

Examine the front view of the skeleton in Figure 1.1. Place one finger on the anatomical name at the top left side of the front (anterior) view of the skeleton where it says sternum. Say the name aloud to help you identify the bone and then place your hand on your own sternum for a tactile reference for this bone and its location in the body. Repeat this process for each of the anatomical names provided. Then repeat this process identifying the skeletal features on the back (posterior) view. The tactile process of mapping each bone enhances your sensory awareness and proprioception skills that support dance training.

Mindfulness in Daily Life: A Shift in Habit

Functional Awareness uses the strategy of reflective practice to heighten awareness of personal movement habits. This method of reflection combines basic anatomical imagery and mindfulness in action.

Begin to discover how your "suit fits." What did you notice during the exploration of hand clasp, arm cross, and leg cross? These choices are not wrong or bad. There is no value judgment placed on what you notice. It is merely an unconscious pattern of movement. Everyone has habits of asymmetry. We invite you to let go of the labels of "good" or "bad" and instead investigate whether the movement choice is useful or effective depending on the context. Awareness of these habits and choosing when they are necessary enhance postural health. Recognize how you are positioned in your body and practice releasing unnecessary tension. Consider letting yourself move out of habit and into a state of curiosity about balancing the body differently. We invite you to keep a movement journal where you can practice using the anatomical names of the bones as you record your findings. This journal can help you notice patterns over time.

2

Dynamic Alignment and the 4Rs

How we stand affects how we dance. Conscious awareness of this daily activity can enhance patterns for neuromuscular balance. Unconscious habits may place unequal force on the body's structural integrity as well as unnecessary stress on joints and muscles. The simple act of standing invites an opportunity to promote dynamic alignment and improve dance skills.

The Story: How We Stand

John, a tall gentleman in his late 40s, came to see me because he had severe and chronic back pain in his lower back/lumbar area. He had surgery involving spinal fusion. This surgery provided a temporary relief, but after a while his pain returned. I explained to John that, as babies and toddlers, our standing balance is well organized with little unnecessary effort. Over time, we start to accommodate to our surrounding environment. For example, tall people may slouch down to accommodate to a chair that is too small. As people move into the teenage years there are psychophysical adaptations that are often made unconsciously. A teenager may think that he is too tall and intentionally slouch. Someone else may feel too short and try to lift his chin to appear taller. These postural habits develop a mis-stacking of the skeletal structure and undue pressure on the spinal vertebrae. John's surgery attended to the compressed disc but did not address a potential source of the original issue. His long-standing posture remained, so the body continued the habit of creating pressure on the spine.

During this explanation to John, he exclaims, "Oh! I know where this habit of standing comes from! When I was a boy there was a show called My Three Sons, *and at the start of every show they had the three sons standing there with one son leaning onto one leg, arms crossed and tapping his foot during the theme song. The teenage boy, Rob, was so cool on that show. I remember when I was 10, I said to myself 'I am going to be cool and stand like Rob!'"*

John's revelation, about when he began standing lurched to one side, helped him understand the unconscious movement pattern he had developed (Figure 2.1). Recognizing this habit enabled him to make new choices toward balance and relieve his chronic pain. You may not have an "aha" moment, yet it is possible for everyone to begin developing self-awareness and recognizing patterns in stance.

We first learn to stand as toddlers. Developmentally healthy toddlers exhibit elegant and efficient balance with little unnecessary effort. As children grow, stimuli from the surrounding environment influence their posture and movement choices. Humans naturally mirror those around them, whether in conversations with friends or by

Functional Awareness. Second Edition. Nancy Romita and Allegra Romita, Oxford University Press.

imitating current popular body postures. These interactions affect overall body stance. Environmental influences that adversely affect standing posture include wearing backpacks, long periods of sitting in chairs, and maladaptive sleeping positions (Noll, 2017). One of the beautiful attributes of the human body and brain is the ability to adapt and change. One strategy to enhance self-awareness, prevent injury, and improve dance techniques is learning how the body works through functional anatomy.

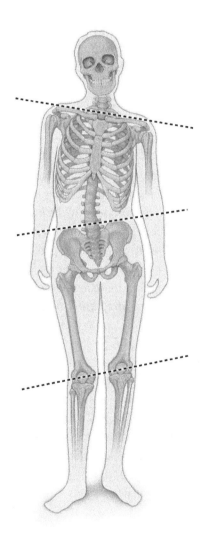

Figure 2.1 John's posture

The Anatomy: An Introduction to Skeletal Center of Gravity

The skeletal system can balance in standing with minimal stress to the neuromuscular system. If you are standing with your center of gravity (COG) aligned, as shown in Figures 2.2 and 2.3, the body's musculature is balanced and there is minimal stress on the system.

Unconscious posture habits move the COG into imbalance, causing stress or increased force on the neuromuscular system. When the system is not balanced through the COG, the center of pressure shifts, muscles overwork, and the resulting uneven skeletal alignment increases stress on the vertebrae and joints. Look at the line through the middle of the body of the skeleton depicted in Figure 2.2. This line is often referred to as the plumbline of balance in the sagittal plane. The mid-sagittal plane equally divides the body into right and left halves. If you stand and throw the weight of your body onto one foot more than the other, you create an imbalance in the neuromuscular system.

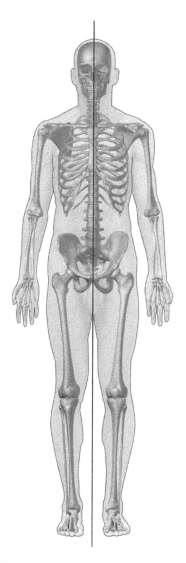

Figure 2.2 Skeletal front view

Look at Figure 2.3. The line identifying the frontal or coronal plane separates the body into front and back halves. If the head juts forward out of alignment with the spine, or the weight on the feet shifts back onto the heels, the COG moves. This results in an imbalance in the neuromuscular system that leads to muscle fatigue and discomfort.

Figure 2.3 Balanced standing side view

Exploration: Center of Gravity

Try a movement experiment to experience this shift in COG for yourself.

1. Stand with feet in a parallel position, toes facing forward, and feet about hip-width apart.
2. Shift your weight forward mostly over the balls of the feet. Hold this position for a moment.
3. Do you feel tension or gripping in your body? Where do you sense this extra tension or effort?
4. Shift the support in your feet so most of the weight is now back on the heels, with the toes still on the floor. See how far you can lean without falling off balance, then hold this position for a moment.
5. Do you begin to feel tension or gripping in the body? Where do you sense this extra tension or effort?

During dance class, the body is required to shift weight forward onto the balls of the feet or back onto the heels. This is part of the beautiful expressivity of dance. It is also important for dancers to be able to develop body awareness to perform standing positions in the alignment seen in Figure 2.3. For example, this alignment is important when turning and when traveling through space. Daily unconscious habits for standing compromise the body's resilience and its ability to find the COG in order to balance or turn effectively. Maintaining balanced standing through the COG can prevent injury and improves confidence and emotional well-being. Functional Awareness uses the following four-step method to develop body awareness and to gently encourage the body toward balanced standing.

Functional Awareness 4Rs

Recognize

Stand for a moment. Imagine you are waiting in line at the grocery store. Move into a comfortable, familiar place in which you like to stand. Are you leaning forward on the balls of your feet or back on your heels? Notice if you are standing on one leg more than the other. Notice if one foot is ahead of the other or one foot/leg is turned out more than the other.

Release

Release unnecessary tension. This second R is your opportunity to let go of needless muscular tension, and of unnecessary mental tension or judgment around what you are noticing.

Recruit

Recruit a new movement choice or a new way of being. In Functional Awareness, we recruit through anatomical visualizations. Throughout the remaining chapters, we will provide many anatomical visualizations to help you to recruit a new way of being.

Restore

Restore toward balance. This step does not require effort. Balance is dynamic. Balance is task specific. Balance is ever-changing. It is constantly being defined and redefined depending on the task at hand. Balance is not a station to arrive at but rather a manner of traveling (Figure 2.4).

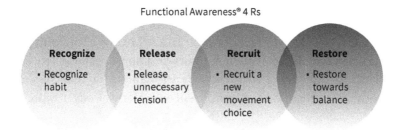

Figure 2.4 Functional Awareness 4Rs

The Anatomy: The Tripod of Balance of the Foot

The movement experiment described earlier, shifting weight toward the balls of the feet and then back onto the heels, demonstrates the importance of the feet in determining balanced standing. Many people think of the foot as one lump that fits into a shoe. The foot is a complex structure composed of 26 articulating bones. In addition, the foot contains several sesamoid bones (bones embedded in tendons) to provide shock absorption or cushion for the ball of the foot. With 26 articulating bones and 31 joints, we have many choices for how we stand on our feet.

Easeful balance is often achieved if the foot is resting evenly through three points of contact. These landmarks are called the tripod of balance of the foot. Anatomically, the first landmark rests between the distal heads of the first and second metatarsals. The second point of reference is between the distal heads of the fourth and fifth metatarsals. The third point in the tripod of balance is located at the anterior calcaneus between the lateral and medial malleoli. Figure 2.5 helps you to visualize these landmarks of balance on the bottom of the foot. If the feet are balanced through the tripod, the body will redistribute force through the rest of the body and reduce unnecessary muscular effort.

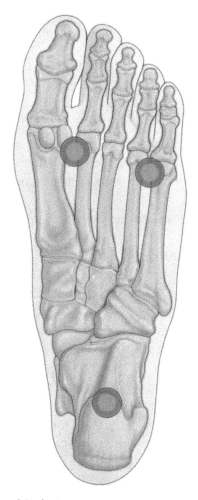

Figure 2.5 Tripod of balance of the foot

Postural control is the body's ability to control its position in space through the synergy of sensorimotor input and action. Balance can be defined as the ability to control one's center of mass in relation to the base of support and maintain equilibrium. We can discover balance in relative stillness as well as dynamically while moving. Both static and dynamic balance are required in the training and performance of most dance forms. Balance is a complex movement organization that requires many body systems including the vestibular, proprioceptive, and visual systems. Considering the anatomical visualization of the tripod in each foot can help us move out of habitual stance and toward balance. Both balance and postural control are important in developing motor activity competence because they provide the basis for stability and orientation during a movement task.

Take a moment to bring awareness to your feet. It does not matter if they are on the floor, a leg is crossed, or you are reclined while reading. Look at Figure 2.5 and think about the three points in the right foot. Think of the tripod of balance points in the left foot. This mental practice of anatomical visualization during quiet moments supports the brain-to-body patterning development for more rigorous moments in dance class.

Exploration: Finding Your Feet

This simple exploration applies gentle pressure to the soles of the feet. In this way your customary stance for balance becomes unhabituated. It then releases unnecessary tension and allows the foot to discover the tripod for balance with ease.

1. Take one or two athletic socks and roll them up in a ball—or you can use a small, soft ball.
2. Place the sock under the right foot so it is about in the center of the arch.
3. Now move both feet forward onto your toes and lift the heels off the floor. Then rock back onto the heels, rolling gently through the pressure of the sock. Repeat this several times.
4. Take the sock out from under the right foot. Does the right foot feel different from the left? For some it may feel odd; for others, it may feel more stable; and for some, it may not feel very different at all. All of these experiences are valid and helpful in terms of letting the body move out of habit and into awareness.

Repeat Steps 1 to 5 with the sock under the left foot. Notice whether there is a change.

Mindfulness in Dance Training

Discover some habitual movement preferences while dancing. Do you favor using one leg to turn over the other? Do you prefer one leg as your standing leg during a one-legged balance? While watching a teacher demonstrate a combination, do you find yourself leaning onto the same leg most of the time?

The Functional Awareness approach to becoming aware of habit is one that invites curiosity and a sense of fun. It is not "bad" to stand on one leg more than another. The discoveries we make about unconscious movement habits are neither bad nor good. A question to consider when you find yourself leaning onto one leg might be, "Is this useful at this moment or does this position compromise my stability?"

Mindfulness in Daily Life

Over the years, students have asked for information on how to stand for long periods of time, as the body seeks a balanced relationship between exertion and re-cuperation. If you are chopping vegetables at the kitchen counter, waiting in line, or chatting at a social gathering, consider the 4Rs and the tripod of balance to prevent fatigue. The body appreciates small, frequent adjustments to maintain a dynamic alignment.

The Anatomy: The Balance of the Head

The anatomical visualization of the tripod of balance of the foot is one effective strategy to discover the center of gravity during balance since it addresses an awareness of where the body contacts the ground. At the opposite end of the body, the head balances on the spine. The skull has a profound influence on dynamic alignment. The adult skull generally weighs between 10 and 12 pounds. There are seven vertebrae in the neck or cervical spine. The first cervical vertebra is called the atlas. Just as the Greek god Atlas held up the entire world, this first cervical vertebra holds up the skull, which contains the brain, our world of ideas and thinking. The atlas or C1 vertebra articulates with the skull at the occiput. The atlas is the pivot point to nod yes. Beginning the "nod" action at this place produces minimal impact on the rest of the spine. (See Figure 2.6.)

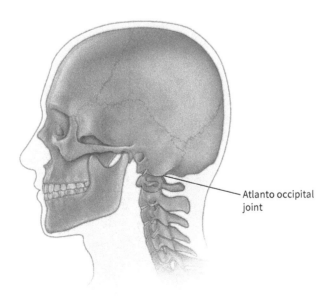

Atlanto occipital joint

Figure 2.6 The atlanto-occipital joint

The spinal column houses the spinal cord, which is the bundle of nerves that travels from the brain through the entire spine. If unnecessary pressure is chronically placed on the rest of the spine by the skull, the nerves can be compressed and cause weakness and pain in the body.

To help visualize the location of the atlanto-occipital joint (often referred to as the AO joint), place your tongue just behind the top teeth on the hard palate. Make a clicking sound with the tongue to sense the skeletal structure just posterior to the upper teeth. Next, slide the tongue back in the roof of the mouth. The texture becomes softer. This to the soft palate. Just beyond the soft tissue of the soft palate, where the tongue can barely reach, is the AO joint. It is located further forward and often higher in the skull than people tend to imagine.

The skull has a large hole at the base (the foramen magnum) to allow the spinal cord and the vertebrae to form the spinal column, thus allowing the spinal cord to disseminate nerve function through the rest of the body. The foramen can be seen in Figure 2.7. The first cervical vertebra (the atlas) articulates at the bony ridge around the foramen called the occiput to form the atlanto-occipital joint (Figure 2.6). If the head is tipped back, it places pressure on the AO joint and the rest of the spine. If the face is pulled forward with eyes down, as often happens when one is using a cell phone, this posture also causes unnecessary stress on the spine. It is simple to discover the correct poise of this joint and to find your natural upright balance in the body.

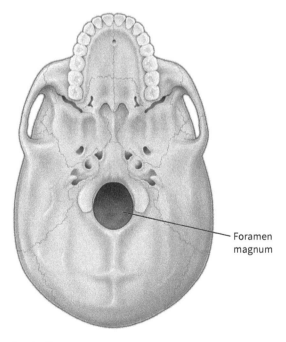

Foramen magnum

Figure 2.7 The superior skull

The amount of physical exertion needed to support the head is minimal when the head remains poised with the ears aligned over the shoulders and hips. If we have a habit of jutting our face forward to see the computer screen or to read this book, the amount of physical stress and energy can be up to three times greater on the system. This action to jut the face forward creates wear and tear on the vertebrae as well as fatigue and overuse in the muscle structure. Additionally, the successful completion of many elemental dance actions depends on this weight being well balanced on the spine. If the head juts forward when turning or balancing, the body uses more effort and force to complete the movement. This effect can be observed in the middle and right-hand images in Figure 2.8.

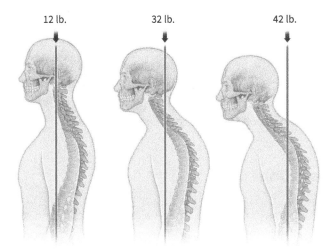

Figure 2.8 Effect of head posture on the spine

Exploration: Discover Integrity of Balance at the Atlanto-occipital Joint

The following exercise was inspired by the work of Alexander Technique teacher, Judy Leibowitz.

1. Place one finger on your chin, then take the other hand and place one finger on the occipital ridge, which is the base of the skull.
2. Let your eyes gaze at the horizon, then begin to pull or crane your head forward, then pull it back and tuck the chin in. Notice the muscle effort in this experiment.
3. Finally, allow the body to restore toward balance. With your fingers maintaining contact with your chin and skull, discover a place where the head and neck feel in more easeful balance.

4. Let the head to remain easefully balanced as you read. Play with tipping the skull gently from the AO joint without also craning the rest of the neck.

Without judgment, notice your head position at this moment. Remember there is no wrong or right posture. Merely recognize what is. Ask yourself to release unnecessary tension in the neck.

Mindfulness in Dance Training

When the head is not aligned over the spine, the COG is pulled off the plumbline of balance. This in turn leads to unreliability for a clear turning axis. It is harder to balance and more difficult to execute multiple turns when the head is forward. Your ability is compromised for vertical height during quick small jumps and during large jumps and leaps. The head position is stopping you from achieving your optimal height when jumping. It is very difficult for the body to suddenly align the head during the middle of a dance phrase if most of the day you are craning the head forward while looking at your cell phone or computer screen.

Mindfulness in Daily Life

When using your phone, periodically take a moment to notice and reflect on the balance of your head in relation to your spine (Figure 2.9). Consider rebalancing your head in an easeful manner and discover what feels balanced. It is a bit funny to think how frequently we hold the phone and then bend our head and body down to look at messages. It is a mobile phone. We have the option to move it easily by bending our elbows to bring it closer to the face to read.

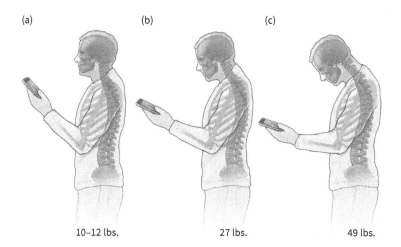

| (a) | (b) | (c) |

10–12 lbs.   27 lbs.   49 lbs.

Figure 2.9 Effect of cell phone use on spine

3

Impact of Thinking on Doing

The use of imagery in dance education has an illustrious lineage. Mabel Todd, a pioneer in kinesthetic anatomy, wrote an innovative book in 1937 entitled *The Thinking Body*. She had studied body alignment and patterns of coordination as early as 1926. Her work is important in relation to somatic work and dance training. Lulu Sweigard worked with Todd and developed studies in ideokinetic imagery. Irene Dowd followed with her inspiring book entitled *Taking Root to Fly*. These innovative philosophies on teaching dance were integrative, linking the domain of the intellect with the realm of the body.

As founder of the University of Wisconsin's dance program in 1926, Margaret H'Doubler professed the philosophy that dance technique "must be experienced in a way that recognizes the anatomical, physiological, and psychological connections and disciplines" (1998, p. 96). This somatic-based philosophy on dance education inspired Nancy Topf during her study with H'Doubler at Wisconsin. Topf's "repatterning technique" works with kinesthetic imagery as a tool for alignment, awareness, and exploration of movement vocabulary. Eric Franklin is a writer and teacher of the 21st century, providing strategies for the application of imagery to the teaching of dance techniques. These somatic pioneers, among others, have inspired dance teachers to aid students toward improved performance and body understanding through imagery.

Recent research substantiates the premise that merely thinking about something changes the body's skeletal and muscular response. Thinking has a pivotal relationship to dynamic alignment and balance.

The Story: Chips the Dog

In a modern technique class offered at Towson University's Burdick Hall dance studios, my students and I decided to try this informal experiment. The students were performing a jump activity in pairs. One student informally measured the height of the jump of her partner, using the lines provided by the cinderblock wall behind them as a reference point.

Next, I told the following story about Chips the dog: On Sundays, my husband and I would drive to my in-laws' house outside New York City for a delicious meal of pasta with a red meat sauce. They had a miniature beagle named Chips. Each week we walked up to the front door and rang the doorbell. Chips would scurry to the door,

Functional Awareness. Second Edition. Nancy Romita and Allegra Romita, Oxford University Press.
© Oxford University Press 2023. DOI: 10.1093/oso/9780197586815.003.0004

barking. There was a window on the top portion of the door. Chips jumped to try to see who was at the door. She would jump and jump and jump effortlessly, ears flying up for minutes until someone unlocked the door.

Figure 3.1 Chips jumping

Chips had what is called ballon in ballet technique, the appearance of lightness while jumping. The students imagined Chips and then repeated the jumps while continuing to think of the image of Chips and her head and ears flying up as they performed a few easy jumps. The students repeated the jumping exercise while the partner observed. By envisioning Chips, each student demonstrated a quantitative, measurable improvement in the height of their jumps.

The use of imagery is a powerful teaching tool. Mental imagery and mental training can have a profound effect on the body to elicit or prevent improvement in dance skills. Changing your thinking can change your dancing.

Exploration: Thinking Up and Thinking Down

1. Stand tall with your feet hip distance apart. Imagine that your whole body is filling with heavy wet cement from the top of your head all the way down to your feet. Take time to sense the cement weighing down on each structure of the body. The head sits heavily on the neck. The wet cement sloshes around in your ribcage to fill all of the spaces between each rib. The ribs sink under the weight of the cement onto the pelvis. The bowl of the pelvis fills with the dense liquid and sits heavily on the legs. As the cement continues down each leg, imagine it spills out the soles of your feet and fills the room so that you are in cement up to your ankles—and then the cement hardens. From here, try jumping a few times while maintaining the image of the cement.
2. Make note of the sensations you experienced and your ability to jump while embodying this image.
3. Shake that off.
4. Stand tall once again. Now imagine that your head and chest are a hot-air balloon. The side-body is like the strings and the pelvis is the light woven basket

attached to the balloon. Imagine lift off! You, as the balloon, float up, up, up, and away! At this point, try jumping a few times while maintaining the image of the hot air balloon.

5. Make note of the sensations you experienced and your ability to jump while embodying this image.

Your Findings and Why They Matter

When you are thinking down (cement), the body responds and the action of jumping can become cumbersome. When thinking up (balloon), the body accesses the deep postural support system and the body can move with more ease in jumping.

In the 1960s, NASA scientists were focused on the space race to the moon. During the Apollo missions with three astronauts in the capsule, the astronauts were in a weightless environment for longer and longer periods of time. The astronauts would return to earth by splashing down in the ocean. The astronauts were carried out in huge cargo nets onto a ship. Once on board, it became apparent that they could not stand! It took up to a week for some of them to regain standing balance. This led the support team to think there was muscle atrophy in space, so they designed ways for the astronauts to maintain large group muscle function through resistance training. The astronauts prepared for the next mission, flew into space, and returned; they still could not stand up after the return from the weightless environment in the space capsule. The team finally realized that a group of postural support muscles very close along the spine are autonomic. These muscles support the spine in an upright posture as a natural "righting system" for balanced movement. They contain muscle fibers, rich in mitochondria, which enable them to function constantly and effortlessly for long periods of time, but they require a trigger: gravity. In response to gravity's force down, these muscles engage to support the body in upright posture. Hence, gravity is not a force weighing us down; it is the impulse for us to stand up!

The Anatomy: Muscles of Postural Support

The deep postural muscles help us interact with gravity in a resilient fashion. If we interfere with these deep stabilizing muscles, the much larger muscles of the back begin to execute the muscular effort required. One can perform the task of upright posture with the larger, more superficial muscles, but this requires more effort, uses much more energy, and the muscles become fatigued more quickly. The body experiences this fatigue as tension or pain.

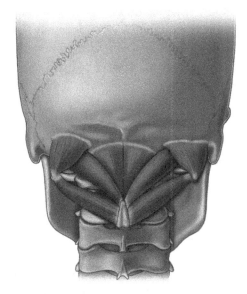

Figure 3.2 Suboccipital muscles

The muscles illustrated in Figure 3.2 are known collectively as the suboccipital muscles. These muscles are predominantly local stabilizers. If the skeletal system is in balance, these local stabilizers can work autonomically and tirelessly to maintain balance of the head and neck.

Figure 3.2 illustrates the four specific muscles of the suboccipital group: the rectus capitis posterior major and minor and the obliquus capitis superior and inferior. They are short muscles with limited mobility. They aid in extension, side bending of the cervical spine, and limited rotation at the first and second cervical vertebrae (nodding yes and no). These muscles function constantly and subconsciously to maintain spinal balance while we are sitting, standing, walking, and dancing.

In addition to the suboccipital muscles, another primary muscle group for postural support is the transversospinalis. The transversospinalis group is comprised of three sets of muscles that are very deep along the spine and run superomedially from the transverse process to the spinous process. The rotatores span one vertebra and are closest to the spine. The multifidus muscles span three vertebral levels and lie just superficial to the rotatores. The semispinalis are the most superficial muscles of the transversospinalis group and spans five or six vertebral levels. These muscles aid extension, flexion, and rotation depending on their responses to other muscles, but they are pivotally important for upright posture. Together this group of muscles form a strong "braid" or chevron along the spine to allow for spinal mobility and postural stability (Figure 3.3).

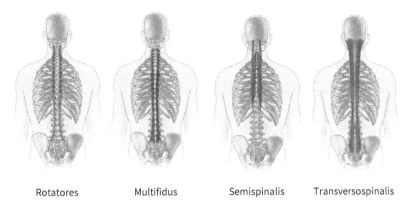

Rotatores   Multifidus   Semispinalis   Transversospinalis

Figure 3.3 Transversospinalis muscle group

Understanding the inherent muscle structure to support a lengthening spine is necessary for discovering efficiency of movement and freedom from unnecessary effort and tension. As dancers, we often think that demonstrating effort is a good thing, but unnecessary effort can impede expressivity. If the body is balanced through the center of gravity, the muscles of the transversospinalis fire easily and tirelessly. The pull downward from gravity elicits the response for these muscles to support the skeletal system upright. You were experiencing this ease of motion when considering the imagery of the hot air balloon. Gravity, pulling us to the earth, provides a trigger for these muscles to activate and sustain us in dynamic alignment.

Exploration: The Transversospinalis Muscles

Place your arms at your sides with hands resting so that the third finger faces your leg at the side seams of your pants. Take a moment to envision the poise of the head, the balance at the tripod of your feet, and the plumb line of balance through the ears, shoulders, hips, and ankles. Extend your fingers towards the ground to enhance the pull of gravity and then "think up" to engage the transversospinalis. You may feel a sensation of the spine lengthening energetically. Thinking up enables you to recruit the deep postural support system and the body moves with more ease and efficiency.

Mindfulness in Dance Class

Many exercises in dance training begin with a musical preparation. During these moments of preparation, *think* of the tripod of the feet and "think up" through your whole spine. There is no need to push or pull to create the action of "up." Simply by changing your thinking, the body and transversospinalis will engage to naturally lengthen and support the spine in upright balance.

Mindfulness in Daily Life

When carrying grocery bags from the store, distribute the weight of the bags evenly between your two hands. As practiced in the previous movement exploration, "think up" as the weight of the bags pull down. This counterbalance between gravity and energy improves dynamic alignment and the whole health of your back.

4

Motions of the Trunk and Use of Spiral

The spine moves in a myriad of complex ways to fulfill the demands of artistic expression. The balance of upright posture is an excellent place to begin to discover principles that support efficiency in the movement required for any dance aesthetic. Sensing a connection from the head to the pelvis facilitates a crucial organization to allow spirals, twists, and various movements to unfold through the torso. There are tremendous benefits in exploring ways to enhance movement potential in the motions of the spine.

The Story: Dancing for a Lifetime

It was a warm summer evening in New England. We were in a black box theater at Dean College in Franklin, Massachusetts. At 75 years old, master dancer, choreographer, educator, and performer, Bill Evans, performed not just one but two solo works on the program. When onstage, his body exudes a litheness that belies his years. He moves through the space with connectivity and expressivity that draws you into the smallest gesture and surprises you when the movement darts through space (Figure 4.1).

He embodies the resiliency and elasticity inherent in the spiral nature of our neuromuscular system and transforms the movement from "steps" into art. During much of his career, he has been in a deep practice of embodied anatomy and somatics-based dancing. His practice inhibits limitation and permits possibility.

Bill Evans embodies the inherent design of the possible movements in the trunk. The human body is not composed of straight lines and right angles. The bones of the body are strong and resilient because each has an inherent spiral or curvature. The resilient nature of the spine, the supporting musculature, and the myofascial system afford the body a wide variety of choice in movement. Exploring movement activities along with anatomical information enhances the awareness of body functioning, and the body can release habitual holding and tension that impede movement potential. The following exploration reveals information about the range of motion available in the spine.

Functional Awareness. Second Edition. Nancy Romita and Allegra Romita, Oxford University Press.
© Oxford University Press 2023. DOI: 10.1093/oso/9780197586815.003.0005

Figure 4.1 Bill Evans

The Anatomy: Spinal Curves

The spine has several sections, and each one has a slight curve that provides resiliency in the structure for adaptive movement. The cervical, thoracic, lumbar, and sacral sections contain curves that support the range of movement of the torso. The seven bones of the neck are called cervical vertebrae. The 12 thoracic vertebrae each have costal bones or ribs that attach to the articular facets on the transverse processes of each vertebra. There are five lumbar vertebrae that compose the lower back. The fused bones of the sacrum create the end of the spine along with the 1 to 3 fused bones of the coccyx comprising the inferior tip at the tail bone. When viewed from the side, the spinal column has four curves. The cervical spine curves slightly anteriorly (forward). The thoracic spine curves slightly posteriorly (backward). The lumbar spine curves anteriorly and the sacrum curves slightly posteriorly. The curves provide a range of motion between flexion and extension in the torso. The different curvatures possible in the spine are illustrated in Figure 4.2.

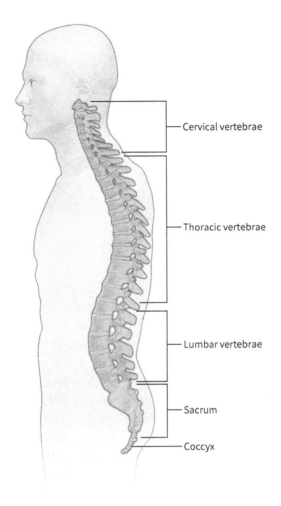

Cervical vertebrae

Thoracic vertebrae

Lumbar vertebrae

Sacrum

Coccyx

Figure 4.2 Sections of spinal column

Lordosis is the curve of the spine that typically develops in the cervical and lumbar spine. Hyper-lordosis is a term used for curves beyond the normative, commonly referred to as swayback. The term kyphosis is used to describe the spinal curve in the thoracic spine; hyper-kyphosis presents as a hunched or rounded back. Scoliosis is an atypical lateral or transverse curvature of the spine. With scoliosis, the spine curves to the side and each vertebra also rotates on the next one in a corkscrew fashion (Figure 4.3).

(a) (b) (c)

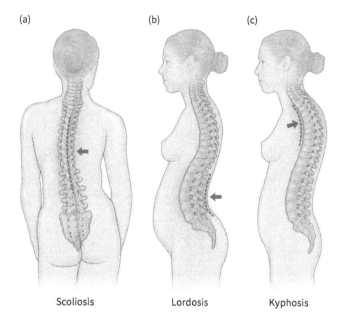

Scoliosis Lordosis Kyphosis

Figure 4.3 Skeletal considerations for the spine

If one section of the spine has excessive curvature, the balance of resiliency is shifted and the body develops patterns of overuse and tension. In some cases, these curves are a genetic feature and passed down through families. This condition is called idiopathic scoliosis or idiopathic kyphosis. These conditions require medical guidance and at times might require surgery; however, these conditions can be mitigated with exercises, braces, and mindfulness to daily habits. These curves may also develop as a result of postural habits and overuse. This condition is called postural scoliosis or postural kyphosis. These conditions can be changed through attention to daily movement habits and reconditioning of the muscles of the trunk to support a balance in the spinal curves.

Dancing is an effective activity for many people with such spinal conditions because most dance classes involve practicing movement experiences in every plane of motion. This supports bilateral neuromuscular training to encourage healthy spinal expressivity. Understanding your body and spinal preferences can help you maximize the potential for movement within the aesthetic you perform.

The Anatomy: Actions of the Spine

There are four actions of the spine: flexion, extension, lateral bending, and rotation. Dance forms combine these movements in delightfully creative ways. Developing a non-judgmental awareness of where your spine moves easily and where it resists movement can open up the possibility of changing this pattern to allow for greater ease and potential for movement. It is important to differentiate between the different actions of the spine in order to embody integrity in each action.

Exploration: Discovery of Spinal Preferences

Spinal Roll Down from the Wall: Flexion and Extension

1. Lean with your back against the wall and your heels a few inches away from the wall. Place your feet a comfortable distance apart and in parallel. Begin to roll down. Instead of rolling down by moving away from the wall, try pressing each vertebra or part of the spine into the wall and then roll down, bringing your head towards the floor. Consider the image of the inside of a wave as it crests. This movement allows the body to sense the spine: where it articulates easily with the wall and where it moves in chunks away from the wall.
2. Gently bend the knees and keep them slightly bent as you roll back up the wall, seeing if you can feel the vertebrae connecting back to the wall.
3. Repeat Steps 1 and 2 once more. See if you notice any difference in your overall contact with the wall and in the dynamic elasticity of your back.
4. Now, step away from the wall completely. Perform a spinal roll down without the wall for support. See if this spinal articulation is now different from your habitual manner of rolling forward.

Side Bending Right and Left: Lateral Flexion

1. Once again along the wall, with the legs in a wide stance and arms overhead in a wide V, how far can you bend to the side? Can you bend the same amount to the other side? Does the sensation of stretch on the side of your body feel equal on both sides?

Spiraling: Spinal Rotation Right and Rotation Left

1. Step away from the wall and place your feet in a wide parallel position. Consider the tripod of balance at the feet and the balance of the AO joint.
2. Close your eyes and turn your head and spine to the right, letting your arms wrap around your torso.
3. Open your eyes and see how far you have turned.
4. Now repeat to the other side. Is it easier to turn your head and spine in one direction than the other?

Your Findings and Why They Matter

Asymmetrical, unconscious habit can create stiffness and lack of mobility in specific areas of the spine and torso over time. For example, if you always sleep with your head turned to the same side, those many hours in one position create a predilection to turn to that side and a comparable restriction of movement on the other side over time. If you always tuck one knee up tight to your chest when sleeping, this position creates an imbalance in the lower back. Such imbalanced rotation for long periods of time during sleep has an effect on the ability to rotate more efficiently in one direction than the other.

Mindfulness in Dance Class

Just before class starts, practice roll down from the wall, side bending at the wall, and the rotation sequence from the movement exploration to discover the flexibility of the spine. This practice includes letting go of the assumption or expectation that this will be the same each time. Some days we have more range of motion than others. The task is to recognize and attend to our spines and bodies as they are. After class, let your spine discover neutral from the rigors of class by rolling down from the wall or lying in a neutral spine on the floor in semi-supine (on your back with your knees bent).

Between exercises in class, consider the tripod of the feet and balance of the head, aligning the curves of the spine, and recovering from the joys and demands of twists, turns, side bending, and contractions required in class. It is a moment to pause and restore toward balance.

Mindfulness in Daily Life

Getting out of a car or out of a chair each day is a delightful place to engage in the elegant use of the spiral muscular for ease in action. Remember that the spine starts up at the AO joint, let your eyes and head lead the turn and let the whole spine follow. Allow your spine to simply rotate, without flexion or extension through the spine. Let the torso freely move around the spine and press the feet into the floor to help propel you out of the chair.

"Getting it right" is not the point, rather it is about the opportunity to bring your attention to spiral movements during daily tasks, making the mundane playful and fun. To find integrity in the spine, one must be able to differentiate between the actions. Purposeful action of the spine creates a potential for full expressivity within whatever dance aesthetic you are performing.

5

Core Support

Take a moment to reflect on your personal understanding of core support. What exercises, if any, do you practice frequently to address core support? Where are these muscles? Close your eyes to rest from reading and reflect on what you currently know about the core.

Core support is the skeletal, muscular, and myofascial recruitment needed to maintain a balanced center of gravity (COG) in any position. Core support involves coordinated alignment and multiple muscle actions. Core support can often focus on stabilizing the pelvis and abdominal region. This particular focus on the pelvic region is a very important aspect to core support, yet it is not the whole story.

The Store: Core Support and Postural Control

In high school and early college, I was a competitive gymnast. I was taking dance classes while also in the gym training for performance on the balance beam and uneven parallel bars. My favorite event was the uneven parallel bars. The action of glide kips requires a strong abdominal core. The muscles of my abdomen, back, and pelvis were well conditioned and defined. Hundreds of repetitions of various sit ups and abdominal exercises were part of my daily routine. Cross training information suggests core exercises help prevent injury and support trunk stability, yet oddly I was in chronic, sometimes significant, low back pain. After various visits with medical professionals and trying several somatic movement training modalities, I realized I was missing an extremely important piece of the puzzle for core strength and stability: global postural control. All my hard work in the training room for abdominal strength and pelvic stability was being undermined because I was focusing solely on the individual muscles but leaving out the integration of the strength building in relation to the central stability through the whole body.

Core support enables the dancer to balance, jump, twist, lift, and turn. Core support is vital for dancers to maintain health and wellness while engaging in the rigors of training and performance. The Functional Awareness approach to movement proposes that core support also relies on a series of global postural support systems. These factors are not a separate feature of core support; rather, they are integral to the

Functional Awareness. Second Edition. Nancy Romita and Allegra Romita, Oxford University Press.
© Oxford University Press 2023. DOI: 10.1093/oso/9780197586815.003.0006

understanding of core support. Global postural control attends to stabilization of the body as a fully integrated system. Several factors contribute to this comprehensive, strong, and resilient support: skeletal alignment, strength of the muscles of the pelvis and trunk, and neurocognitive practices all help to maintain balance and control. There are many excellent programs for conditioning the body and strengthening various muscles considered to comprise core support. Functional Awareness practices develop greater sensory and cognitive understanding for the conditioning of core musculature through mental training and practice.

Mental imagery, a type of mental training, can be defined as imagining without physical execution. Mental practice is the act of imagining oneself executing an action. This practice is a training method by which mental imagery is used to improve performance prior to or after performing the action. Strategies in mental practice integrate body systems to support the muscular exercises associated with core strengthening to improve stability (Castagnoli et al., 2015; Slimani et al., 2016). Coupling mental training and practice with physical training can enhance strength performance and global postural control. Thinking fundamentally affects doing.

Imagine the core of an apple (Figure 5.1). Think of central support like the core of an apple providing support from the floor of the pelvis to the roof of the mouth. This image can be utilized as mental training to develop neurocognitive skills for global postural control.

Figure 5.1 Core of an apple

The Anatomy: Visualizations

Visualizing anatomical landmarks as a practice of mental training can deepen access to the core as a whole-body system for support.

Tripod of the feet: The feet are a long way from the trunk of the body, yet the balance of the feet in relation to the earth has a significant effect on the effort required through the rest of the trunk to maintain controlled balance. The body navigates responses based on where our feet meet the ground. While reading this sentence, examine how the image of the "core of the apple" is supporting you in your current position. Consider the position of your feet even if you are seated or reclined. Recognize this and ask yourself to release unnecessary tension. This is a general request and the body might let go of tension in the low back, jaw, or feet. Now, readjust the feet to support you through the tripod landmarks in each foot. The feet do not have to touch the floor to consider the tripod. Let your thinking establish a relationship between the feet and your central support.

Balance of the AO joint: The position of the head in relation to the torso also influences central stability and the integrative organization of core support. One of the muscles at the most superior portion of the "core of the apple" is the palatoglossus muscle, commonly referred to as the soft palate. Mapping the atlanto-occipital (AO) joint as an anatomical visualization helps to facilitate dynamic alignment of the spine. Visualizing the soft palate as one of the muscles supporting global postural control for the core helps integrate the functions of the head, neck, and tongue with the abdominals and the muscles of the pelvic floor.

Sternum/pubic bone: Imagine that there is a ribbon between the inferior end of your sternum (the xiphoid process) and your pubic bone (pubic symphysis). Splay your ribs and tip your pelvis to make the ribbon very taut, and then move into more of a slump in your spine to make the ribbon slack. As you move through extension of the spine acknowledge how those two points are moving farther from each other, then when you move into flexion, they are closer to one another. Move through an exploration of extending and flexing through the spine to then discover a placement of your ribcage and pelvis that allows the ribbon to lie flat.

Anatomically, you do indeed have a ribbon-like structure, called the linea alba. This is a strong fibrous fascia that connects the sternum to the pubic bone. This appears as the white line down the center of the torso in Figure 5.2.

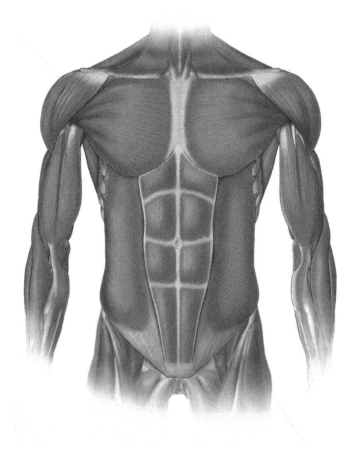

Figure 5.2 Superficial muscles of the torso

This connection between the sternum (xiphoid process) and the pubic bone (pubic symphysis) provides a useful visual image for postural control. The linea alba consists of connecting fibers for some of the key muscles of the trunk needed for core strength.

Mindfulness in Dance Class

At the beginning of class, take a moment to let mental practice set up your experience for the class. Imagine the tripod of balance of the foot, then consider the relationship between your xiphoid process and the pubic symphysis. Visualize the soft palate as a reference point to balance the head on the spine. Remember, this is not a practice of *doing* something but a practice of permitting your *thinking* to activate global postural support.

Mindfulness in Daily Life

Before you go to sleep, lie down on your back with knees bent in a semi-supine position. Imagine the central core of the apple, the relationship of the sternum to pubic bone, and the soft tissue of the roof of the mouth at the soft palate. Simply thinking these images before bed helps you develop neurocognitive patterning for integrity of the central support.

The Anatomy: Muscles of the Abdominal Core Support

It is useful to learn the muscles required for core support, their location, and how they can be used to enhance the potential for success when you are performing dance skills.

The transversus abdominis encircles the torso from the back near the lumbar spine (at the thoracolumbar fasciae and costal bones 7 to 12) and wraps around to the front of the body and attaches along the whole front of the torso, along the strong fibrous sheath of the aponeurosis of the linea alba. The transversus abdominis, whose fibers run horizontally, creates a girdle to support the torso from ribs to hips. It also has fibers that interconnect with the diaphragm. The transversus abdominis is one of the primary muscles you can feel when you cough. Place your hand on your belly and cough a few times. You will feel a muscle pulling in. This is the transversus abdominis aiding the diaphragm to help expel air from your lungs. If you hold it too tightly, it inhibits breathing. If you do not engage the transversus abdominis effectively, your stability in the lower back and pelvis can be compromised.

Superficial to the transversus abdominis are the internal and external obliques. These muscles support side bending and spiral movements of the trunk. The fibers of the internal obliques run in the opposite diagonal direction of the external obliques.

The most superficial abdominal muscle is the rectus abdominis. This muscle originates at the xiphoid process and travels along the front of the abdomen to the pubic bone. The fibers of this muscle run vertically. It is often referred to as the six-pack muscle.

The horizontal fibers of the transversus abdominis, the diagonal fibers of the obliques, and the vertical fibers of the rectus abdominis create a strong multidimensional muscular support system. Together this muscle group is a primary mobilizer of the torso, capable of supporting the body in wonderful actions that require strength and agility (Figure 5.3).

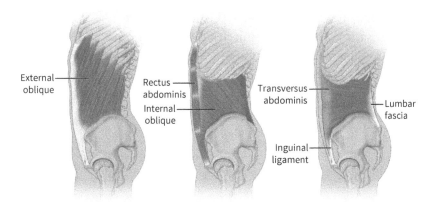

Figure 5.3 Transversus abdominis, obliques, and rectus abdominis

Abdominal exercises aim to strengthen this group of muscles to ensure greater stability for the torso when you are lifting, carrying, or even just supporting your own weight. Plank and side plank are excellent exercises to engage the central support system and develop greater stability through the center/core of the body. Breathing is inextricably linked to the central neuromuscular and myofascial support systems. Holding the belly in too tightly can restrict breathing and impose restrictions on your ability to have a strong central support system for dancing. Excess contraction can promote imbalances in core strength that lead to back pain. One suggestion is to recruit the muscle no more than 30% when navigating dance movements while standing. When you are squatting or lifting, stronger contraction of the muscle is needed to stabilize for the increase in force on the central support system.

The core is a series of muscular layers that work in concert to sustain the body in upright posture, aid in all motions of the trunk, and function to enable efficient lifting, swinging, and partnering. They sustain the integrity of the body in action. The deepest muscles for central support are examined in detail in Chapter 3, the transversospinalis. In carrying over the lessons from the previous chapters, it is important to consider the plumb line of balance to engage core spinal support from the rotatores, multifidus, and semispinalis group on the posterior trunk while the psoas provides deep postural support on the anterior portion of the trunk. Another group of deep support muscles, the muscles of the pelvic floor, are at the base of the pelvis.

The Anatomy: Muscles of the Pelvic Floor

Consider the image of the core of the apple. The pelvic floor acts as the base for this image of core support. The pelvic floor refers to the muscular structure that spans the inferior portion of the pelvis from both the pubic bone and the ilium to the coccyx. These muscles (Figure 5.4) form a supportive hammock for the skeletal pelvic bowl. Maintaining elasticity and resiliency in the pelvic floor muscles is important for several reasons. These muscles control urinary function, so they maintain urinary tract health. The pelvic floor muscles enhance sexual satisfaction as the muscles involved in orgasm. The pelvic floor also provides a hammock of muscular support for the internal organs in the lower abdomen.

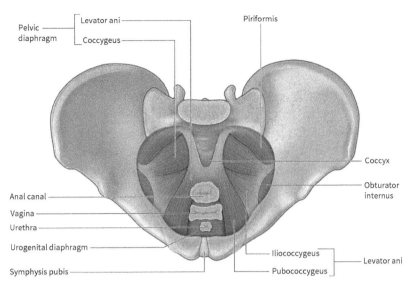

Figure 5.4 Muscles of the pelvic floor

The levator ani, coccygeus, and internal obturator muscles of the pelvic floor are important for dancers because they coordinate with breath to support any action to move the pelvis. The muscles of the pelvic floor are an internal steering mechanism for propelling the body.

Exploration: Sensing the Muscles of the Pelvic Floor

The muscles of the pelvic floor aid in stabilizing dancers in movement. They also regulate the flow of urine out of the body. To begin to feel these muscles and how they work, try this the next time you use the bathroom to urinate. Begin the flow of urine. Stop and hold the flow for a couple of seconds. Let the flow begin again. Repeat this several times. You are activating the muscles of the pelvic floor.

Your Findings and Why They Matter

For some, this activity allows a sensing of the pelvic floor for the first time. For others, this activity may help to refine understanding of the pelvic floor in a kinesthetic manner. You can activate this group of muscles to aid in global postural support during balance tasks and traveling movements.

Mindfulness in Dance Class

Let the anatomical imagery of the pelvic floor and abdominal muscles and your experience with engaging these muscles buoy you during a movement phrase in class. Explore easeful support from these muscles. Do not over-contract. Recruit the muscles for action, but do not grip. Remember it is the natural recruit and then release of muscle fiber that allows for maximum resiliency for dancing. See how this changes your experience with the movement. If asked to pull up in your belly during a standing exercise in dance class, support the transversus abdominis at 30% of its contraction ability. Save the greater contraction of the transversus abdominis muscle for movements that require strength and power. Constant over-engagement restricts action and expressivity instead of enhancing your skill.

Mindfulness in Daily Life

Standing at the sink while washing your hands is an opportunity to consider global postural support. Imagine central stability like the core of an apple—a cylinder of support from your pelvic floor up to the soft palate. The Functional Awareness approach to core support includes central stability for skeletal alignment, muscular recruitment, and mental or neurocognitive practices to maintain a balanced center of gravity in any position. Small frequent mental reminders in daily tasks help to reinforce the patterns within body systems that are then required during the more rigorous practices while dancing.

6

The Pelvis and Hip Joint

The pelvis and hip joint are primary drivers for movement, yet many of us are not clear where the ignition key is located. This story demonstrates the importance for dancers to understand how the pelvis and hip joint function to prevent unnecessary wear during the rigorous requirements of dance training.

The Story: A Ballet Dancer's Unconscious Postural Habit

A talented dancer and dance educator, who performed with American Ballet Theater (ABT) and on the Broadway stage, started to experience chronic pain in her hips while walking, and more and more limitation in turnout during passé, retiré, and développé. She recognized two interesting habits that were having a significant impact on her body. During her everyday actions and in dance class, her toes were always pointing out to the sides as if she was standing rotated in first or second position. Her norm for her hips and legs—and not just her practice during class—was standing and walking while turned out. Ballet is a beautiful art form that requires rigorous hours of practice. However, it is not useful to turn out all day, every day. You might think this constant practice would improve the skill. It turns out there are several factors that affect range of motion in the hip joint. The unconscious, constant repetition of turnout actually interferes with the resilient balance of the myofascial and neuromuscular system surrounding the hip's ability to perform efficiently.

The pelvis is the conduit from the torso to the legs. The femur or thigh bone attaches to the pelvis at the acetabulofemoral joint, commonly referred to as the hip joint. There are several factors that contribute to the range of motion in the hip joint: unconscious postural habit, skeletal structure, excess muscular tension, and ligament laxity.

Exploration: Mapping the Hip Joint

The first factor is an unconscious postural habit and mis-mapping of the skeletal structure. The dancer in the story was unaware of where the hip joint was located and this contributed to her activation of muscles that started to restrict rather than facilitate full range of motion.

Functional Awareness. Second Edition. Nancy Romita and Allegra Romita, Oxford University Press.
© Oxford University Press 2023. DOI: 10.1093/oso/9780197586815.003.0007

1. Point to where you think your femur, or thighbone, meets the pelvis at the hip socket. Make a note of this spot. When asked to point to the hip socket, many people are uncertain where this joint is located. They will point to their greater trochanter, located on the thigh or femur bone, or often people point at their waist at the top of the hip ridge known as the iliac crest.

2. Place your hand on what is commonly known as the hip bones. This is the anterior superior iliac spine (ASIS).

3. Begin to move your hand toward the pubic bone. You will feel a softer space, a hollow or indent. This area is the anterior portion of the ball-and-socket joint of the hip, where the head of the femur rests in the socket called the acetabulum.

4. Leave your fingers here and march in place. You will notice this area folding. This motion is the head of the femur gliding in the socket to allow for hip flexion. For many, the location of the hip socket is a surprising revelation. It is much closer toward the front and center of the body and closer to the pubic bone than most people visualize (Figure 6.1).

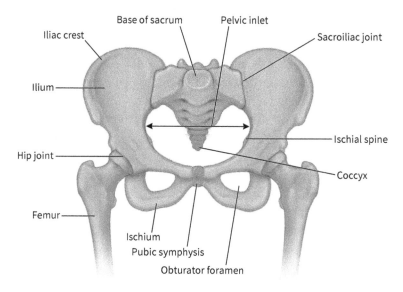

Figure 6.1 Skeletal landmarks of the pelvis and hip joint

Your Findings and Why They Matter

When we have a faulty body map of where a joint action occurs, the brain recruits muscle action based on this inaccurate information, and the body then moves inefficiently. This unconscious mis-mapping of the hip in relation to the leg can create a muscular and myofascial imbalance and contribute to snapping hip syndrome, low back pain, a tight iliotibial band (IT band), or patella tendinitis (jumper's knee). Fortunately, the brain and body are very adaptable. It is easy to rethink and discover a body map with greater structural integrity. Functional awareness of hip rotation and pelvic alignment are key to improving dance technique and maintaining whole body health. Placing your fingers at your acetabulofemoral joint at varying times during the day will help you develop a mental practice to repattern the body's understanding of this hip joint. The ballet dancer from the story shifted away from the habit of chronic turnout by applying this tactile and mental practice.

The Anatomy: Honoring Differences in Skeletal Structure

The second factor that affects range of motion is the skeletal structure itself. There is wisdom in knowing the things we cannot change. The bones that comprise the pelvis and hip joint have the same fundamental design for everyone, but individual variations in shape may affect the range of motion. The images in Figure 6.2 demonstrate several common differences in pelvic skeletal structure. Note that the ilium is taller and more vertical in pelvis A, whereas pelvis B is wider and has an ilium shaped more like a bowl. Do you see the differences in the pubic arch angle? Can you identify other differences?

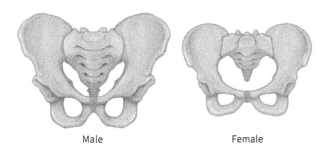

Male   Female

Figure 6.2 Skeletal differences in the pelvis

These differences, which reflect the beauty of the human form, can affect the range of motion in the hip socket. The hip joint, or acetabular femoral joint, is a ball-and-socket joint. The rounded head of the femur bone fits into the concave structure of the acetabulum of the pelvis. A ball-and-socket joint facilitates flexion, extension, adduction, abduction, medial rotation, and lateral rotation.

For some people, the neck of the femur is short (the neck is the portion of the femur that connects the shaft of the femur to the head that fits into the socket) and for others the neck is longer. A shorter femoral neck may make external rotation/turnout easier. Another pertinent skeletal feature is the depth of the acetabulum/socket. For some, the socket is shallow, often allowing more external rotation/turnout. For others the socket is deep and this limits the amount of range that is available to rotate inward or outward (Figure 6.3).

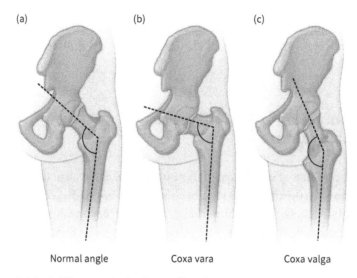

Figure 6.3 Individual differences in the femoral head

The Anatomy: Muscular Considerations for Range of Motion in the Hip Joint

The third factor that affects range of motion is excess muscle tension. This can be inadvertent. Many dancers will try too hard in their efforts to accomplish a desired movement. When we first learn a skill, it is natural to recruit more effort than needed as the body and mind try to figure out how to solve the problem at hand. As you become more familiar with the motion, it is helpful to begin to discern the muscular action that the skill truly requires so you can isolate any excess tension that may be impeding the movement rather than supporting it.

The hip joint has a complex muscular support system. A few key muscles are useful to know for improving dance training and developing resilient muscular balance between stretch and strength. One key support muscle for hip flexion that links the torso to the legs is the psoas major, as seen in Figure 6.4. It is the muscle closest to the spine in the front or anterior side and attaches to the bodies of the vertebrae of the spine. The psoas is the deepest muscle anteriorly and is similar to the transversospinalis muscle because it contains stabilizing muscle fibers to support the body in an upright posture. The psoas muscle interdigitates with the iliacus to form a common tendon called the iliopsoas tendon. The psoas major also contains mobilizing fibers to support movements of dynamic action. It is a strong flexor of the hip and the only muscle that flexes the hip beyond 90°.

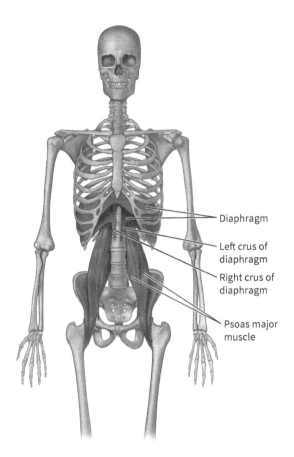

Figure 6.4 Psoas major

Exploration: Releasing the Psoas from Habitual Contraction

1. Stand in parallel. Establish a standing leg and a working leg. Lift and extend the working leg out in front of you toward hip height. Notice the ease or discomfort in the working hip joint during this action. Try again using the other leg.
2. Lie down on your back with your knees bent and feet on the floor in a semi-supine position. Take a moment to allow your body to rest on the floor, letting the body yield to gravity.

3. Place a rolled-up bath towel transversely where the sacrum meets the lumbar spine. This maintains your natural lumbar curve while lying down.

4. Take a few minutes to rest here, noticing your breathing and asking yourself to let go of any unnecessary tension.

5. Slowly extend your right knee to straighten the leg along the floor. Easily slide the leg back to a semi-supine position. This movement is inspired by the Bartenieff Fundamental Pre-thigh Lift. Repeat this action a second time.

6. Extend your left knee to straighten the leg. Easily slide the leg back to a semi-supine position. Repeat this action a second time.

7. Gently remove the towel, and let the low back begin to rest into contact with the floor.

8. Roll gently onto one side in a fetal position. Slowly move to stand.

9. Try the leg extensions again and see if there is any difference in sensation. Record your findings mentally or on paper.

Your Findings and Why They Matter

Releasing the habitual tension of the psoas major can create a more dynamic connection from the feet through the pelvic floor to the head. This muscle is a pivotal muscle for central support and has several key roles in movement function. It supports the body in upright posture, it is a primary hip flexor, and it interdigitates with the fibers of the diaphragm to support breathing. This exploration with the towel releases the tension in the psoas major to create more resiliency and ease in action. It is another way to move out of habit, allowing for greater choice in movement.

The Anatomy: Muscles of the Hip Joint Continued . . .

The primary muscles on the posterior and lateral portions of the hip region are the gluteus maximus, the tensor fasciae latae (TFL), the gluteus medius, and the gluteus minimus (Figure 6.5). They support a variety of functions to support and coordinate the hips and legs in action: abduction, medial rotation, and lateral rotation of the hip.

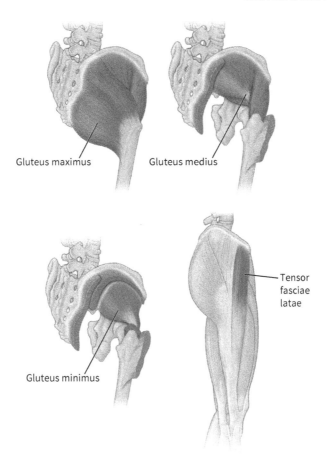

Figure 6.5 Gluteal muscles and tensor fasciae latae

Lateral rotation (turnout) is a specific aesthetic and requirement in many contemporary and classical dance forms. This movement initiates at the hip socket. The biggest muscular misconception for dancers is that practicing turnout all day improves their turnout. They often consciously or unconsciously walk in turnout, stand in turnout, and sleep turned out. This constant activation of one set of muscle fibers without opportunity for recoil and recuperation places increased stress on the ligaments supporting the hip. In short, standing and walking turned out all the time does not improve turnout—it impedes elasticity and resiliency of joint motion. This is the secondary factor in the ABT dancer's hip restrictions and pain. The primary muscles used to recruit turnout in the hip are the deep lateral rotators. The six deep lateral rotators of the hip are the quadratus femoris, obturator externus, obturator internus, superior gemellus, inferior gemellus, and piriformis (see Figure 6.6).

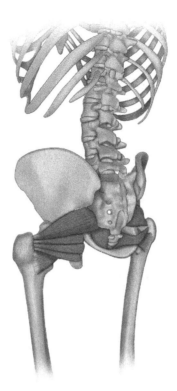

Figure 6.6 Deep lateral rotators of the hip

The Anatomy: Pelvic Neutral

The art form of dance explores (depending on the aesthetic) the end ranges of movement for the pelvis. The muscles that support the pelvis, lower back, and hip joint in action also influence the alignment of the pelvic girdle. Pelvic neutral is a place to maintain or move through, not a position to grip. Gripping or preserving the position of the pelvis with too much tension places unnecessary strain on the ligaments and tendons, resulting in pain at the front of the hips or in the lower back.

Anterior tilt is the anatomical term for the pelvis as it tips forward, which often includes exhibiting a sway in the low back (lordosis). Posterior tilt means the pelvis is tucked under. Try each pelvic position for yourself and exaggerate the sensation.

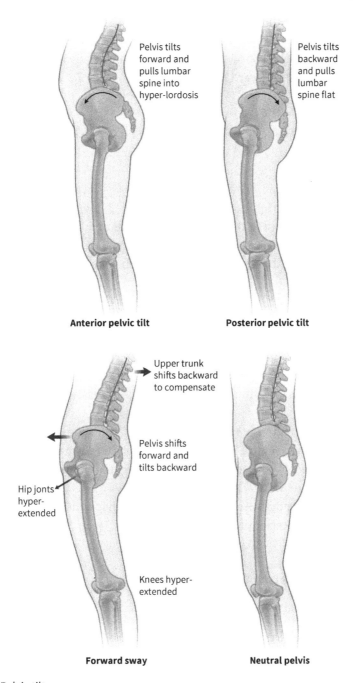

Pelvis tilts forward and pulls lumbar spine into hyper-lordosis

Pelvis tilts backward and pulls lumbar spine flat

Anterior pelvic tilt

Posterior pelvic tilt

Upper trunk shifts backward to compensate

Pelvis shifts forward and tilts backward

Hip jonts hyper-extended

Knees hyper-extended

Forward sway

Neutral pelvis

Figure 6.7 Pelvic tilts

The bottom left image in Figure 6.7 displays a dancer in forward sway. This position occurs when the pelvic center of gravity has been moved too far forward toward the balls of the feet, upsetting the plumb line of balance and dynamic alignment in the whole system. This is a common way for dancers to use the pelvis to shift their weight over the balls of their feet. Unfortunately, this stance places stress on the low back, knees, and anterior portion of the hips. Moving the entire body structure toward equal weight at the tripod of the feet is a more efficient model for dynamic alignment than pushing forward with the pelvis.

Exploration: Anterior Tilt, Posterior Tilt, and Forward Sway

Begin by practicing some of the anatomical imagery presented in the previous chapters. Consider the tripod of balance at the feet. Allow yourself to imagine the balance of the head on the spine at the AO joint. Remember, if you balance at the feet and consider the poise of the head, many unnecessary muscle actions release, allowing you to achieve dynamic alignment with efficiency.

1. Stand with your feet hip distance apart. Bend both knees to allow for more range of motion in your hip joint.
2. Place one hand on the front of your pelvis and one hand on your sacrum. Gently exaggerate into anterior tilt by tipping your tailbone up and dropping the front part of your pelvis toward the floor. Straighten your knees while maintaining this position and notice the any sensations in the lower back and knees.
3. Release into a neutral standing position and softly bend your knees again. Exaggerate a posterior tilt by tucking your pelvis under, as though curling your tailbone between your legs. Once again straighten your knees and note how this tilt impacts lower back, hips, and knees.
4. Explore the range between these two actions. Pelvic neutral is the balanced position between anterior tilt and posterior tilt.

Mindfulness in Dance Class

As you practice a dance phrase during class, be aware of the various movements required in the pelvis. Experiment with pelvic neutral during a phrase that travels across the floor. Investigate the various other pelvic tilts that are possible (anterior tilt, posterior tilt, forward sway). Different dance forms employ many different possible pelvic orientations depending on that style of movement. Observe the choreographer's intention and bring a clarity regarding the pelvis to your dancing. At the end of the exploration in the dance phrase, return to pelvic neutral as well as an awareness of the tripod of the feet and the balance of the head to allow for recuperation and restoration.

Mindfulness in Daily Life

Practicing dynamic alignment in dance class but ignoring it the rest of the day compromises the progress your body can make toward improving range of motion and technical skills in dance training. While brushing your teeth or doing dishes, notice your habitual stance for pelvic tilt. Without judgment, assess this pelvic tilt and gently shift your body toward a balanced neutral. The pelvis is not an isolated structure. As a tool for discovering neutral pelvis, consider the tripod of balance at your feet and the poise of the head before shifting pelvic alignment. When you release the initial habit and recruit necessary muscular support to sustain a dynamic pelvic alignment, you create greater efficiency. Asking yourself to make this pelvic shift in daily use will deepen your motor sensory map for pelvic neutral, and improve your ability to access this pelvic support during dance practice and performance.

7

The Knee

The thigh bone (femur) and the shin (tibia) meet at the knee joint (tibiofemoral joint). The kneecap (patella) rests in front of the femur and tibia (Figure 7.1). The fibula is the smaller bone in the lower leg. This bone is not considered part of the knee joint, but it does act to stabilize the leg and knee. Understanding the function of the knee in relation to the hip joint and the ankle/foot can support the overall health of the knee and improve movement potential during balances, lunges, jumps, and turns.

The Story: Marie's Knees

One Monday morning, a university student asked for a consultation because she was experiencing pain in her right knee during her dance classes. She did not have a specific twisting or falling action that triggered this pain, but it tended to feel less comfortable as class progressed. I asked her if she engaged in rigorous rehearsal or activities over the weekend. "No, I did nothing really active, just worked in a clothing store all weekend." After she recounted her issues, I asked Marie to freeze her body posture and take a moment to consider her standing position. Marie noticed the leg that was bothering her during dance class was now resting in a torqued position. The knee was facing the front of the room while her foot and lower leg were turned out to the side, thus twisting the knee in the joint unintentionally. "Hmmm," she replied, "I wonder if I stood in this position yesterday during my double shift at the checkout register at a clothing store?"

Biomechanical dysfunction is one of the most common contributory factors in patellofemoral pain (Pallaro, 2007). Marie's unconscious torsion in her lower leg is an example of one such contributing factor. One can alleviate discomfort and minimize these factors by deepening understanding of the function of the patellofemoral joint. The knee is a modified hinge. The primary action of the joint is to bend (flexion) and straighten (extension). The knee joint also has a bit of wiggle room as the lower leg can turn in (medial rotation) or turn out (lateral rotation). Such rotation is very helpful in supporting the stability of the leg, adjusting to varying surfaces when standing or walking, and adapting to the actions of the leg while dancing. This ability to rotate inward or outward can also potentially compromise the integrity of the knee joint when used in ways that chronically destabilize it.

Functional Awareness. Second Edition. Nancy Romita and Allegra Romita, Oxford University Press.
© Oxford University Press 2023. DOI: 10.1093/oso/9780197586815.003.0008

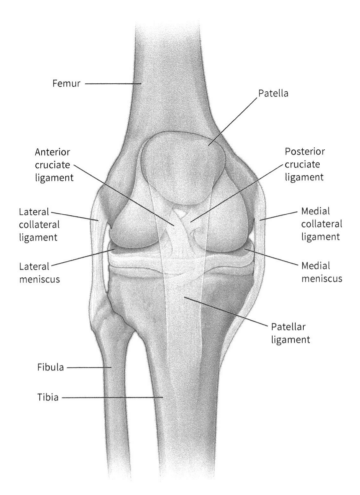

Figure 7.1 Skeletal landmarks and ligaments of the knee

The Anatomy: The Knee Joint

The knee is composed of two joints: the tibiofemoral joint, where the shin meets the thigh; and the patellofemoral joint, where the kneecap meets the thigh. The tibia, femur, and patella are surrounded by a strong configuration of ligaments, tendons, cartilage, and bursas (sacs filled with synovial fluid that lubricate the joint). The patella, a large sesamoid bone embedded in the patellar tendon, protects the tibiofemoral hinge joint. The patella and the patellar tendon act as a fulcrum, a mechanical arrangement that increases the potential strength of the quadricep muscles. The quadricep muscles on the front of the thigh all insert onto this strong tendon to stabilize the knee joint.

The knee functions most efficiently when the femur is aligned with the tibia. This allows the glide of the femoral heads to track within the cartilaginous menisci that cushion the joint when it opens and closes, like the hinge of a door. When the knee is straight, it is very stable and can support the weight of the body as well as any additional force present when you carry objects. When the knee is bent, the hinge is open and provides mobility and potential energy needed to propel the body forward to walk or run.

The ligaments and tendons allow a small amount of lower leg rotational movement (generally 3 to 5 degrees). This range of motion provides the necessary resilience in the knee joint region to adjust to uneven surfaces or change directions while maintaining the stability needed to bend, jump, and lunge. This rotation in the lower leg is referred to as tibial torsion (Figure 7.2). When the lower leg twists or rotates more than 5 degrees, the knee ligaments and patella tendon become strained. This places undue pressure on the menisci, and the cartilage can begin to wear, or the strong patella tendon may drift to one side. This wear and tear puts strain on the joint itself as well as on the ligaments and tendons. Note that the foot is facing outward but the patella or kneecap is still facing forward. The lower leg is twisted in the knee joint so the hinge is not aligned. When the hinges of a door are not aligned the door cannot properly close. This is also true for the hinge of your knee.

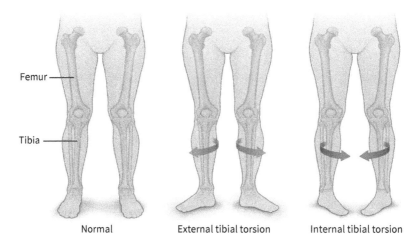

Normal   External tibial torsion   Internal tibial torsion

Figure 7.2 Tibial torsion

Exploration: Awareness in Knee Alignment

Unconscious habits can influence the integrity and stability of the knee joint.

1. Notice the position of your knees as you read. Is a leg crossed over or one lower leg tucked underneath you? Let go of judgment about what you see and sense; simply observe how the knee joint is supporting you as you read. No need to change anything, merely acknowledge your body position.

2. Notice the current position of your knees in relation to the feet. Are they aligned or is your lower leg rotated or twisted in some manner? Release any unnecessary tension you may be experiencing.
3. Permit a moment of reflection to consider whether it might be useful to shift position. Adjust or recruit a different postural organization that you identify as easeful balance for the legs, knees, and feet.

Many dance forms explicitly train dancers to understand that the knee aligns over the feet for efficiency. This is an important and effective method for injury prevention and it helps to develop power in leg action. In daily life, there are no right or wrong positions, yet certain positions provide a mechanical advantage and less strain on the joint system. By periodically bringing gentle awareness to your body positioning, it enables you to make a choice that suits the moment and supports your position in space at that particular time.

The Anatomy: Skeletal Factors Affecting the Knee

One skeletal factor that determines how the knee functions is the placement of the femur in the hip socket and its angle toward the knee. This angle varies slightly from person to person (Figure 7.3).

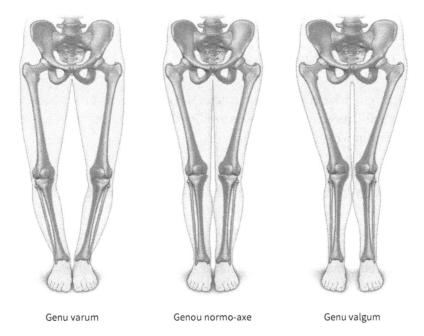

Genu varum   Genou normo-axe   Genu valgum

Figure 7.3 Femoral angle as it relates to the knee joint

When the angle is wide, the knees appear to bow away from each other, particularly noticeable when the feet are close together. This is referred to as genu varum, more commonly known as bowlegged. Genu valgum, the opposite configuration, is commonly referred to as knock knees. In genu valgum, the femur angles inward toward the midline of the body. This particular angle can create strain on the integrity of the knee joint and affect the ability of the knee to take on load or force.

Exploration: Honoring Your Structure

1. Place your hands on the anterior or front location of your hip joint.
2. Stand with both feet directly underneath the hip joints. This varies from person to person. The distance apart may be the width of one fist or two depending on the individual pelvic structure. Place the feet in parallel with the toes facing directly forward.
3. Note the shape of your legs from hip to knee. Then note the shape of your legs from knee to ankle joint.
4. Recognize whether you experience strain or discomfort when standing in this position. Is the strain at the hips? At the knees? At the feet? Record this observation.
5. Permit a moment of awareness to release physical tension or mental expectation. Allow for a breath to consider ease in this position.
6. Adjust your feet and legs for comfort. Note if anything changes with the position of the knee joint and the patella.

Your Findings and Why They Matter

It is useful to understand personal structural configurations in the body in order to differentiate between what are structural considerations and what are muscular factors determining knee joint action.

The Anatomy: Muscular Factors of Knee Stability

Many muscular factors affect the knee. One primary muscle group on the front of the thigh is the quadriceps. The quadriceps muscle group is comprised of four muscles that insert on the patella tendon (Figure 7.4). As you are reading this, place a hand on the muscles of your thigh. Move the muscles around a bit with your hand and note the level of tone. An imbalance in tone can be a muscular factor that contributes to misalignment in the knee joint.

Quadriceps

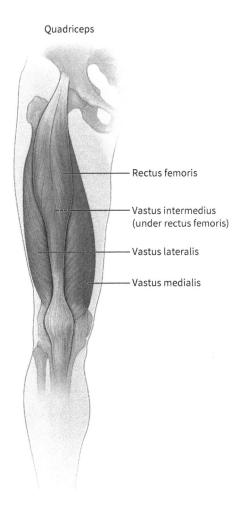

Rectus femoris

Vastus intermedius (under rectus femoris)

Vastus lateralis

Vastus medialis

Figure 7.4 The quadriceps muscle group

The hamstring muscles are three strong muscles on the posterior or back side of the thigh: the semimembranosus, the semitendinosus, and the biceps femoris. These muscles all originate on the ischial bones at the base of the pelvis and insert onto the posterior side of the knee joint (Figure 7.5).

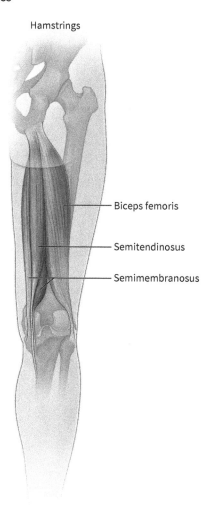

Hamstrings

Biceps femoris

Semitendinosus

Semimembranosus

Figure 7.5 The hamstring muscle group

The hamstrings and quadriceps support the knee effectively when the balance of strength is fairly equal between the quadriceps muscles on the front of the thigh and the hamstring muscles on the back of the thigh.

Exploration: Repattern Integrity of the Knee Joint

This activity examines lower leg alignment with the thigh to develop muscular balance by using the hamstring muscles to support knee joint stability.

Read through these instructions and then try this simple yet effective exercise.

1. Lie on the floor facing down (prone). Place your head on your hands.
2. Bend the right knee and flex the foot while keeping the left leg straight. Lift the right thigh just slightly off the floor. You will feel the hamstring and gluteal muscles as you lift the bent leg. Maintain a parallel position. Once the leg is lifted, lift your head to see your reflection (in a mirror or using a self-view camera) to evaluate whether your lower leg and foot are aligned with the thigh.

3. Adjust the leg to create an integrity of the knee by aligning the lower leg and thigh.
4. If you do this with a partner, they can provide tactile and verbal feedback to support you in this action.
5. Once you've discovered alignment through the leg, lift the thigh an inch or two off the floor maintaining the position, then gently lower it down. Repeat this action eight times to develop muscular balance in the hamstrings to support knee joint stability.
6. Perform steps 2 through 5 on the other side.

The Anatomy: Ligament Laxity and Knee Function

What is hypermobility? Hypermobility is sometimes referred to as hyperextension in dance training. Another common term for this excess range of motion in elbows, knees, fingers, and wrists is "double jointed." Hypermobility is joint laxity or a looseness of the connective tissue in the ligaments that connect bone to bone. Hypermobility is *not* the same as flexibility. Flexibility can be defined as a muscle's capacity to lengthen in order to move a joint (or joints) through its range of motion. By contrast, hypermobility is a laxity in the ligaments that results in an excessive range of motion in the joints. Flexibility resides in *muscle* tissue, while hypermobility exists in the Golgi tendon organs within *ligaments* and tendons. Although flexibility is associated with hypermobility, they are distinct; it is possible to have tight muscles and still be hypermobile.

While flexibility is useful in dance training and performance, general joint hypermobility is *not* required to be successful in the aesthetic movements of dance. Yet dancers commonly utilize the range of motion available to them through hypermobility instead of relying on flexibility alone. An example of how this may present itself in the knee joint is depicted in Figure 7.6.

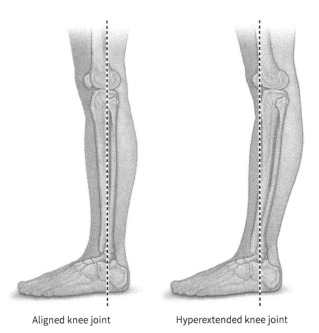

Aligned knee joint   Hyperextended knee joint

Figure 7.6 Ligament laxity in the knee joint

Exploration: Assessing Mobility in the Knee Joint

1. While seated on the floor, straighten your leg in front of you. Record whether your knee joint extends beyond 180 degrees. One knee may be slightly different from the other. Make a note if there is a difference.
2. Stand in profile to a mirror or self-view camera in parallel position. Note whether the knee joint pushes back behind the line of your ankle joint. The leg may even look a bit bowed to the posterior or back. Note whether one leg differs from the other in shape.
3. Recognize "what is." Sense the body and how it is organized at this moment. Release unnecessary tension. Think of the tripod of balance at the feet. Consider the balance of the head at the top of the spine. Note if this shifts the balance of the knee joint.

Your Findings and Why They Matter

The leg is straight when the knee joint is in anatomical extension. There is a natural locking mechanism also known as the screw home mechanism that secures the hinge of the knee in this closed kinetic chain. This ensures an efficient transfer of force through the joint. Some teachers suggest a slight bending at the knee if students are hypermobile in the knee joint. We propose that the anatomical visualization of the tripod of the foot helps to support a strong balanced leg. There is no need to micro-bend the knee joint or make accommodations. If the load at the feet is balanced through the tripod the force transfers through the knee joint to allow the leg to engage its natural locking mechanism. When the knee is slightly bent, the locking mechanism is not engaged and the effort to sustain stability in the standing leg or to stabilize when landing from a jump becomes more challenging and effortful.

Mindfulness in Dance Class

Notice your standing position when observing the teacher perform an exercise or phrase. Are you unwittingly in tibial torsion of the leg? Is the foot pointed one way while the patella is facing another direction? Consider moving out of habit and toward balance in the knee joint.

Mindfulness in Daily Life

Over the next few days gather up some personal data about your use of legs, hips, and knees in daily activities. Investigate and explore your standing and sitting positions and consider the relationship of your knee to the lower leg.

8

The Ankle and Foot

Of all the overuse injuries sustained in dance, 50% are ankle or foot injuries (Conti & Wong, 2001). Investigating the structure and function of the ankle and foot can provide a foundation of understanding to prevent injury and improve resilience.

The Story: Your Feet and Ankles

Think about a story relating to your feet and ankles. Perhaps it is an ongoing "story," or perhaps there is a specific event around the ankle or foot that you remember. Consider your relationship with your feet and ankles. It might be about an injury or the personal conversation you have with yourself when working on specific dance techniques. Take a moment to reflect and perhaps write down a note or two about the thoughts that come to mind on this.

Exploration: Discovering Habit in Feet and Ankles

1. Note the position of your feet. Without shifting or changing, notice the placement of your feet and ankles. Notice without judgment; simply assess the situation.
2. Does one foot have more weight on it than the other? Are both feet on the floor? Is the weight distributed evenly? Is one foot or ankle more turned or rolled in or out? Are you sitting on one foot? Is a leg crossed? How does this affect the shape of the foot and ankle?
3. Release unnecessary tension in your body. Recruit a new movement choice that serves your position and encourages ease and stability in the feet and ankles. Allow yourself to readjust for comfort. Shift away from your habitual stance and restore toward what feels more balanced.

The ankle and foot provide the structural base of support for standing, walking, and dancing. Conscious awareness of distributing the load of the foot develops the foundation for stacking the skeletal structure toward balance (Figure 8.1).

Functional Awareness. Second Edition. Nancy Romita and Allegra Romita, Oxford University Press.
© Oxford University Press 2023. DOI: 10.1093/oso/9780197586815.003.0009

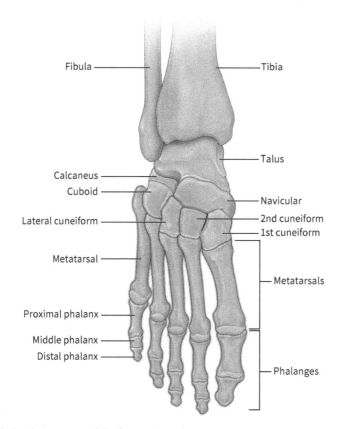

Figure 8.1 Skeletal structures of the foot and ankle

The Anatomy: The Ankle and Foot

Many people unconsciously think of the foot as a singular object at the end of the leg; in fact, the foot and ankle contain 26 bones, 33 joints, 20 intrinsic muscles, and more than 100 ligaments! In addition, the foot has small sesamoid bones (bones embedded in tendons) to provide shock absorption for the ball of the foot. The 26 articulating bones in each foot provide dynamic resilience to bear weight while standing, propel the body through space, and articulate for artistic expression.

The ankle is a true hinge joint. The talus bone rests above the calcaneus (heel bone) and articulates with the tibia and fibula to form the ankle joint. The ankle joint allows the foot to flex, an action that is anatomically referred to as dorsiflexion. This hinge joint also aids in pointing the foot. Pointing the foot is anatomically referred to as plantar flexion because the plantar side or underside of the foot is curling or flexing. This sturdy hinge joint transfers force from the feet upward to the torso or from the leg down to the foot.

The other foot joints perform the additional actions of the foot. The tarsal bones are the bones between the ankle and metatarsals. The metatarsal bones connect the tarsal bones to the toes or phalanges. When dancers use the phrase "circle the ankle around," the movement is performed by multiple joints, creating the action of a foot moving in the shape of a circle. These bones below the ankle joint enable the ankle area and the foot to invert/supinate or evert/pronate. In dance, we refer to this as rolling out and rolling in.

This movement of inversion and eversion is functionally beneficial when you are standing or walking on uneven ground. However, if this action is a chronic habit, it can compromise the integrity of the ankle joint. The uneven distribution of weight caused by unconscious inversion or eversion can lead to weakness and potential injury to the ankle or foot; 85% of all ankle sprains in dancers are inversion sprains/rolling out of the foot (Leiderbach et al., 2008). Visualizing the tripod of balance can stabilize the structure in action to prevent injury (Figure 8.2).

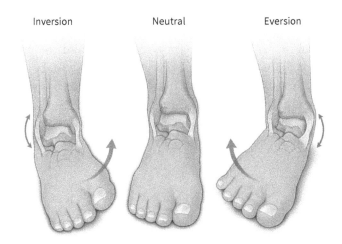

Figure 8.2 Inversion and eversion of tarsal bones

Exploration: Inversion/Eversion

This standing exploration employs the practice of exaggeration as a strategy toward further self-discovery of foot balance. Exaggeration can heighten proprioception and provide the body with additional sensory feedback to reveal personal habits. Be gentle when moving your body through these actions. The activity is less about the rigor of the action and more about learning to sense an imbalance in the feet.

1. Stand up. Begin by recognizing your standing habit. Notice how the weight is distributed in your feet. Does the weight feel balanced? Is one foot bearing more weight than the other? Is the weight more toward the inside or outside of the foot? Are you supported equally through the arches of your feet? Are you rolling in (eversion)? Are you rolling out (inversion)?

2. Supinate (invert) both feet by shifting your weight further toward the outside edges of your feet. How does this feel in the rest of your body? Where does tension build or lessen? Is it familiar?

3. Shift weight to pronate (evert) or move the feet to roll inward. How does this feel in the rest of your body? Where does tension build or lessen? Is it familiar?

4. Rock to the outside and inside edges of your feet a few times to find a centered place. What occurs in the rest of your body to maintain balance in this place?

The Anatomy: Arches of the Foot

The arch is one of the most robust geometric and architectural structures. Each foot has a series of domed support structures: the medial longitudinal arch, the lateral longitudinal arch, the anterior transverse arch, and the posterior transverse arch (Figure 8.3). In addition, the bony arches in each foot provide dynamic support when the foot is load-bearing. The skeletal structure of domes, the neuromuscular system, and the fibrous connective tissue called the plantar fascia support the actions in the lower leg and foot. These actions enable the body to store and expend energy to propel the body forward to walk or move upward to hop, leap, or jump.

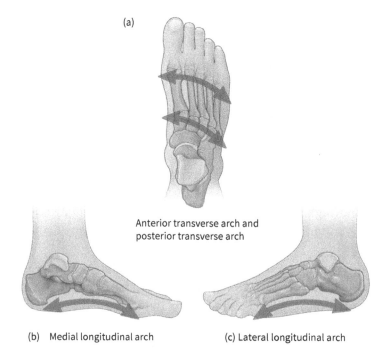

(a)

Anterior transverse arch and posterior transverse arch

(b)   Medial longitudinal arch   (c) Lateral longitudinal arch

Figure 8.3 Arches of the foot

The configuration of the 26 articulating bones in the foot can determine various differences in the arches of the feet. Many people are familiar with the arch you see when looking at the medial or inside of the foot. This arch is called the medial longitudinal arch. There are many genetic differences in the configuration of the bones of the foot, providing a wide variety of differences in the shape of the various arches. Common misconceptions about the arches of the foot are that a low arch is not effective in load-bearing and high arches are optimal. Each of these structural arrangements can provide benefits and challenges in movement. How you manage the use of the structure is more pivotal than the overall skeletal component or "look" of your foot.

Minimal stress to the foot and ankle occurs when the weight of the body is distributed evenly through the whole foot, whether your arches are high or low. Creating the appearance of an arched foot by leaning to the outer foot or gripping at the toes forms an imbalance and weakness in the foot and ankle and can cause discomfort and weakness. Work within the construct of your foot with conscious muscular activation that balances the tripod in action.

Exploration: Tripod of the Foot Revisited

Take this time to review and deepen your understanding of the anatomical visualization of the tripod of balance of the foot and reinforce your understanding of the foot's anatomy.

1. The first point of the visualization is between the distal head of the first and second metatarsal (Figure 8.1). Touch the space between the distal heads of the metatarsals. They can be felt on the top of the foot and then mirrored on the bottom of the foot near the big toe pad.
2. Next, feel the space between the distal heads of the fourth and fifth metatarsal (the fourth and pinkie toe).
3. The third point of reference is at the anterior portion of the calcaneus or heel bone. Feel the medial and lateral malleolus; these are the knobs on either side of the ankle commonly referred to as the ankle bones. Trace a line from these bones to underneath your foot as if making an imaginary stirrup. Your tripod's third point of balance is at the center of the heel bone.
4. Repeat this tactile mapping of the tripod points on the other foot.
5. Finally, place both feet on the floor while seated and visualize these reference points. There is no need to push into the points of the tripod of balance muscularly. Conscious thought is enough to incite a response in the body to move toward a more balanced ankle and foot structure.

Your Findings and Why They Matter

The anatomical visualization of the tripod provides a stable foundation for aligning the skeletal structure during static and dynamic balance. The stability through the arches of the foot can provide support in all actions. In most dance forms, the feet and ankles are essential for the expressivity of the aesthetic. For example, the average ballet class executes 200 jumps per class—more than a basketball player jumps during an entire game (Leiderbach, 2008; Orishimo et al., 2014).

The Anatomy: Muscular Considerations to Stabilize the Foot and Ankle

Many muscles support the lower leg, knee, ankle, and foot. For example, the tibialis posterior and the fibularis longus are two muscles on opposite sides of the lower leg that crisscross and insert on the sole of the foot, creating stirrup-like support for the ankle joint (Figure 8.4). A tendency toward inversion or eversion can compromise the balance of stability of these two muscles in the lower leg. Visualizing the stirrup-like structure of the tibialis posterior and fibularis longus can enhance the recruitment of the muscular support required for balance and provide stability.

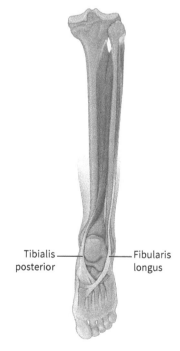

Figure 8.4 Tibialis posterior and fibularis longus muscles

Exploration: Stabilizing the Ankle and Foot

1. Stand in front of a mirror with feet parallel so you can see your ankles and feet. Once you are settled, lift your heels to come up onto the balls of your feet.
2. Look in the mirror and notice whether your ankles are rolling in or out. Then note what you observed and lower your heels down to the floor.
3. Release or let go of any unnecessary tension.
4. Try it again. But this time, visualize the fibularis longus and the posterior tibialis as if they are a stirrup supporting the ankle from both sides. Slowly lift your heels, maintaining a balanced ankle joint. Observe yourself in the mirror to help stay on track.
5. Note whether the visualization shifted the action or the sensation of moving into plantar flexion while standing.

Mindfulness in Daily Life

Similar to the movement exploration at the beginning of this chapter, when you are sitting in a chair for some time, it may be useful to be aware of how you prefer to arrange your ankle and foot. Are they balanced through the tripod of the foot? Are the two feet symmetrical? Your unconscious habit may contribute to imbalances in foot and ankle strength that cause discomfort or pain. Over time, begin to discern if there is a relationship between how you sit (in terms of the lower leg and foot), how you stand, and how you dance.

Mindfulness in Dance Class

The next time you find yourself between movement exercises while a teacher demonstrates an exercise or phrase, notice your habits for your foot and ankle stance. If you sense an imbalance, recognize what is happening and release unnecessary tension in the body and mind. Then envision the weight evenly distributed using one of the anatomical visualizations from this chapter, such as the foot's four arches, the muscular stirrup of the fibularis longus and posterior tibialis, or the tripod of balance. In this approach of anatomical visualization through reflective practice, we invite you to consider balance, not as a station one arrives at, but as a way of traveling. Balance is not one position. Instead, it is a manner of being that shifts from moment to moment in lively response to the environment.

Many strategies exist to find foot balance and dynamic alignment within many dance aesthetics. We are proposing that this anatomical image of the tripod of balance and sensory awareness of the points of load through the foot is an image that can support any aesthetic requirement. The moment the body entertains the visualization of the tripod, the body rights itself in moving toward balanced function.

9

Walking and Weight Shift

Walking is a shift of weight from one foot to the other, propelling the body's center of gravity through space. We can also walk backward for a moonwalk or shift weight from one foot to the other by traveling side to side as in a grapevine step. In dance training, the transfer of weight occurs in many directions. These transitional movements deeply affect expressivity within the performance of dance. Our unconscious movement habits can unwittingly interfere with the ability to transfer weight. Weight shift affects the ability to run, turn, or leap successfully.

The Story: The Cobbler

I live in Brooklyn, New York. In the city, it is common for people to take more than 10,000 steps per day. With that much walking, anyone would need to send their shoes to a cobbler. This is why there are shoe repair places all over New York City. I have a pair of boots that I love. I continually need the soles replaced, so I can continue to wear them even after I've worn them out. On my third trip to replace the heels of my boots, Victor, the cobbler, pointed out that I am constantly wearing out one spot on my left heel more than the rest. Aha! This was a useful observation, since I regularly have left ankle pain and discomfort. My shoes were a clue to what my habit was in walking and the reason for my discomfort in my ankle. I strike heavily on the outside of my left heel more than my right. Thanks to Victor, I have a better understanding of what my habit is in shifting weight from one to foot to the other during the daily practice of walking.

Take a look at the bottom of your favorite shoes. Where are they worn out? Does this reflect where you keep your weight in walking and standing? The shoes can be clues to walking patterns and your preference for how you shift weight from one foot to the other.

We learn to walk when we are very young, yet we are never taught how to do so biomechanically. Movement patterns can form even while babies begin to crawl and walk, and these patterns affect our skeletal structure, muscle structure, and myofascial tissue. Walking, like standing, can promote balance, or it can systemically develop patterns that can be a source of imbalance and compromise ability to shift weight while dancing.

Marika Molnar is an innovator in the field of dance medicine and dancer wellness. She is a physical therapist who has supported dancers of all styles and forms for over 40 years. Marika is the director of physical therapy services to both the

Functional Awareness. Second Edition. Nancy Romita and Allegra Romita, Oxford University Press.
© Oxford University Press 2023. DOI: 10.1093/oso/9780197586815.003.0010

New York City Ballet and the School of American Ballet in New York City. She provides instruction and guidance in gait repatterning with every patient regardless of their injury. "Walking, aside from breathing, is probably the most common activity we all do as human beings and bi-pedal movers" (Molnar, personal communication, August 25, 2021). When examining how a patient walks, Marika looks for asymmetry or imbalances in weight bearing. The following exploration can help develop an awareness of walking patterns and how they might affect how you dance. It is also a delightful resource for creative movement invention.

Exploration: Stepping into Someone Else's Shoes

This activity can be performed in pairs with one person as the leader and the other as a follower. You can try it on your own by following the instructions for only the leader. The leader initiates the movement and the follower mirrors the actions of the leader.

1. Leader: Begin by standing in a comfortable stance.
   Follower: Take a moment and observe the leader's body stance from a side view and then from the back or posterior view. Stand behind them and mirror the body positioning.
2. Leader: Begin walking around the room. Notice what part of your body leads the action in walking. Is the face or head the first body part to move forward and break the vertical plane? Do the hips push the body forward to travel? Do the feet lead? The chest and ribs? There is no judgment in what you discover. Enjoy and continue walking in this manner.
   Follower: Imitate or mirror the walk of the leader.
3. Leader: Notice asymmetry or idiosyncrasies about your walk today. Start to exaggerate these so they become evident to the person following directly behind you.
   Follower: Take on these new exaggerations.
4. Leader: Amplify the exaggeration some more. At this point your walking will not resemble the way folks ordinarily walk down the street. Permit the exaggerations to be directly related to your idiosyncratic habits of walking.
   Follower: Embody these new exaggerations.
5. Leader: Stop leading and step away.
   Follower: Continue walking as if you were following the leader. Perform this movement for a time, so the leader can observe the exaggerated habit in weight shift.
6. Discuss your findings with each other. The leader speaks first, then the follower speaks of their personal experience afterward.

Your Findings and Why They Matter

Small unconscious habits create subtle imbalances in walking. We may not feel them during the day, but the repercussions from these habits affect the system over time. If you walk for 5 minutes in an exaggerated manner of your habit, you may reveal the muscle stress that would occur in regular walking over the course of an entire day. This movement exploration demonstrates the muscular impact your habits have on the body. One exploration performed on one specific day does not explain your habits of walking, but it can provide insight into your gait. These insights supply an opportunity for you to explore awareness while walking during the rest of your week. Walking can be an effective recuperation tool and whole-health activity. If you have an issue with walking patterns and you walk a lot each day, this issue is repeated, and the imbalances that accrue over weeks, months, and years will have an impact. So, working consciously on gait can be one of the best possible recovery tools for the body.

Exploration: Weight Shift

1. Find a method for shifting weight forward and back from one leg to the other that is familiar to you in a particular dance form you enjoy. Let the arms move or swing easily as you move from one leg to the other. Perform this several times, then shift so the other leg is in front and repeat.
2. Notice what part of your body likes to initiate or lead this action.
3. Repeat this process with weight shifts in the frontal/coronal plane, moving side to side.

Is there any correlation or connection to how you move through this weight shift and when you are traveling through space while walking? There may be some similarities or there may not. This activity is meant to help you collect clues or information about your personal preferences for traveling through space.

The Anatomy: Biomechanical Considerations in Gait

Each person has a unique walk, and there is no single set of tips to address everyone's issues when coaching gait. It is useful to become functionally aware of a few key points within gait to elicit greater ease and balance. Mindfulness can aid the body in recuperation from activity instead of contributing to imbalanced action that fatigues the body further.

Gait cycle

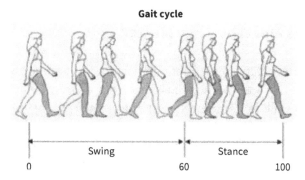

Swing   Stance

0   60   100

Figure 9.1 Phases of the gait cycle

The gait cycle begins when one foot strikes the ground in front of you and it ends when the same foot strikes the ground again. There are two phases in gait: the stance phase and the swing phase (Figure 9.1).

Stance phase occurs when a foot is in contact with the earth. This phase includes the initial heel strike of the foot in dorsiflexion on the ground, a rolling through the weight of the foot; and then propulsion off the ball of the foot in plantar flexion to propel the leg to begin to swing forward.

Swing phase occurs when the foot is not in contact with the earth and the leg is literally swinging from extension to flexion. Once the foot propels off from the back, the leg swings freely to travel forward.

This seemingly simple motion involves the whole body from heels to head. Flexion and extension occur at the ankle, the knee, and the hip. Rotation occurs as a ripple effect up the spine. Flexion and extension reverberate into the shoulder joint to create the swinging of our arms. There are many places throughout our body where we can unwittingly create grinding, pulling, twisting, straining, or misalignment during gait. As soon as the leg moves into slight medial or lateral rotation and does not track efficiently, strain is put on the entire leg structure. As indicated in the story that opens this chapter, you can sometimes see idiosyncrasies by looking at the bottom of your shoes that you wear most frequently while walking. These habits can facilitate ease of motion or they can compromise the system.

Exploration: Ease in Walking

1. Stand with equal weight on both feet. Consider the tripod of balance at the feet and gaze out at eye level to visualize the AO joint and poise of the head. Think up, not down.
2. Slightly shift your weight to the right leg as you peel your left foot off the floor and propel or push off the ball of the left foot. Continue to pedal from one leg to the other.

3. When walking efficiently, the knee is the first body part to break the plane forward—not the face, feet, pelvis, or ribs. Take several steps considering the knee leading (Figure 9.2).

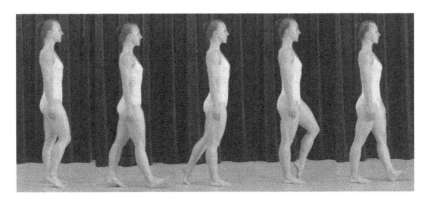

Figure 9.2 Exploring phases of gait

The most common issue for people who experience pain from walking and running is their over-stride—taking steps that swing too far from the body's center of gravity. Try smaller steps at a quicker tempo when you are in a hurry instead of large steps that overexert the system.

Mindfulness in Dance Class

Large traveling steps and leaps require that you propel the back foot to shift the weight forward. Many leaps require a dynamic alignment from head through pelvis so the whole body travels easily through space. During a traveling phrase across the floor, notice what part of the body leads. What is your habit for initiating the movement? Can you recognize what is occurring, release unnecessary tension, and rethink the movement initiation required for that phase?

Mindfulness in Daily Life

On your way to dance class, allow the many joints of the lower limb to bring you to your destination. Let the knees lead or break the plane forward as you propel off the back foot. Notice the rhythm of your foot strike. Is the rhythm even from left to right or do you favor one side more than the other? Think about an even rhythm and see if it allows the body to become more symmetrical.

The Anatomy: Fascia and Its Role in Walking and Weight Shift

Fasciae are bodily structures consisting of fibrous tissue that are primarily composed of water, collagen, and proteins. The system of myofascial tissue known as the superficial back line runs from the forehead along the eyebrow line to the top of the head and travels along the neck, the back, and sacrum. This long chain of connective tissue then continues down the back of the thigh, behind the knee and the calf, around the heel to the sole of the foot to the toes. It literally connects the head to the foot.

At times, portions of this connective tissue can become sticky and less resilient. The lack of glide between fascia and muscle can contribute to muscle tension. Releasing the tissue with gentle pressure can provide greater ease. Walking and weight shifts are a whole-body action, so releasing the superficial back line can help reorganize the body and coordinate the systems that support locomotion. Sometimes the soles of the feet carry unwarranted tension and the fascia is not able to navigate smoothly. A gentle tactile release can help realign the foot as well as shift whole-body organization during weight shift.

Exploration: Fascia Release of Superficial Back Line

Part 1

1. Sit in a chair or on the floor. Find a position where you can easily reach your left foot with your right hand.
2. Make a gentle fist shape with your right hand
3. Begin at the distal heads of the 1st and 2nd metatarsals or the big toe mound and rub with your knuckles in a gentle rolling fashion to release the skin and the fascia just below the skin.
4. Move your fist towards the 4th and 5th metatarsal and perform the same rolling action along the lateral longitudinal arch.
5. Gently apply a cross rubbing action at the base of the calcaneus or heel and continue this cross-fiber gentle rubbing along the Achilles tendon.
6. Repeat steps 1–5 on the other leg, using the left hand in a gentle fist to rub the right leg

Part 2

1. Bring your fingertips to your forehead just above your eyebrows. Lightly make small circles to rub along the forehead from the center out to above the ears.

This is a gentle touch to release the tissue just below the skin. No need for deep massaging here.

2. Continue to rub from the top of the scalp down to the base of the skull or occipital ridge to release the fasciae along the back of the neck

3. Travel down to the sacrum or base of the spine. Give your body a slightly more vigorous rub in this place.

4. Finally, brush along the hamstrings at the back of the thighs and then along the back of the calf to the Achilles.

5. Stand and take a walk around the room. No need to think or do anything in particular. Note whether the legs and body feel different about traveling. Reminder: Whatever your experience, it is valid.

Mindfulness in Dance Class and Daily Life

Become aware of how you initiate any transfer of weight. The teacher or dance form may require a specific approach to how weight is shifted from one foot to another. In any moment of walking from one place to another, consider the full superficial back line of fasciae. Allow the knee joint to break the plane of space first as you travel forward while maintaining easeful dynamic alignment through the spine. Purposeful attention to walking has the potential to minimize stress and maximize your abilities to move in versatile ways while dancing.

10

Expressivity of Arms

The movement of the arms is an intricate element of artistic expression in dance. The arm structure has complex skeletal features, joint articulations, and many muscular attachments to the axial skeleton. As a result, a dancer can inadvertently restrict the full range of possible motion through daily patterns or a misunderstanding of the function of the arms.

The Story: To Sleep, Perchance to Dream

An undergraduate dance student mentioned during technique class that they were experiencing restricted movement in the shoulder. They were finding it more and more challenging to raise their arms overhead during activities in class. Physical therapy, specific exercises, and taping the shoulder proved helpful, but ultimately the shoulder was not regaining its full range of motion without discomfort. When asked about sleep position, they explained that they preferred sleeping on their right side in a fetal position. This position rolls the shoulders forward and places strain on the tendons and ligaments (Figure 10.1).

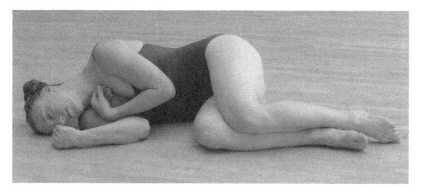

Figure 10.1 Side sleeping position

The movements of the arms are inextricably linked to the actions in the spine. Likewise, an exaggerated curve in the thoracic spine influences the muscle balance in the shoulder structure. I suggested placing a pillow in the front of the student's body from the pelvis to the chest. This simple pillow prop prevented the shoulder from rolling forward during the night. We can develop patterns for making choices in daily action to support dancer wellness and dance training, even in sleep! Purposeful

Functional Awareness. Second Edition. Nancy Romita and Allegra Romita, Oxford University Press.
© Oxford University Press 2023. DOI: 10.1093/oso/9780197586815.003.0011

movement choices can also be applied during waking hours to release unnecessary tension and improve resilience in the shoulders and arms.

The Anatomy: The Skeletal Structure of the Shoulder

The arm structure is part of the appendicular skeleton. It is comprised of the clavicle, scapula, humerus, radius, and ulna. The shoulder girdle is made up of three distinct joints that work together in concert (Figure 10.2). To map the first joint, bring your fingers to the top of your sternum, or breastbone. Feel the heads of the clavicles on either side, where the sternum and clavicle connect. What you are feeling is the sternoclavicular joint, where your arm skeletally attaches to the axial or central skeleton. If you allow your fingers to continue traveling laterally along the clavicle, you'll discover the second of these joints: the acromioclavicular joint, at the top of the shoulder where the scapula meets the clavicle. Then the third joint is the one that we generally refer to as the shoulder: the glenohumeral joint, where the head of the humerus meets the glenoid fossa of the scapula.

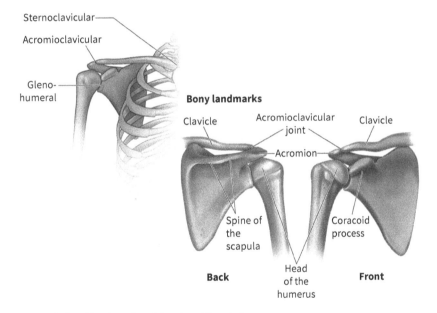

Figure 10.2 Skeletal landmarks of the shoulder girdle

There are seven actions at the glenohumeral joint: flexion, extension, abduction, adduction, medial rotation, lateral rotation, and circumduction. The actions of the glenohumeral joint are aided by the sternoclavicular joint, the acromioclavicular joint, and the movement of the scapula along the torso.

Exploration: Axial Integrity to Support the Appendicular Action of the Arms

1. Sit in a chair near the edge of the seat with your arms resting down by your sides. Let the body slump and sit in a C-curve shape. Rest with your pelvis

curled under in posterior tilt and let the shoulders roll forward as a natural re-sponse to this sitting posture.

2. Slowly, while staying in the slumped position, lift the arms directly forward and then overhead without letting them drift wider on the pathway upward. If you feel resistance, then stop. How does this feel? What do you notice about your shoulders?

3. Let your body undo the slump, release unnecessary tension, and restore toward an upright sitting position that encourages a lengthened spine. Sit on your is-chial bones as you visualize the tripod of balance of your feet and the balance of the head at the AO joint.

4. Once again, bring the arms in front of you and then slowly overhead. How does embodying upright balance in sitting change the experience of this action in the arms?

Your Findings and Why They Matter

What's impinging this action in your arms when in a slouched position and arms are moving overhead? The forward head posture in a slouch affects the thoracic cage or upper back. The head, neck, and thoracic spine positions then affect the shoulder and arm. The alignment in the axial skeleton impacts the range of motion available in the appendicular skeleton (Figure 10.3).

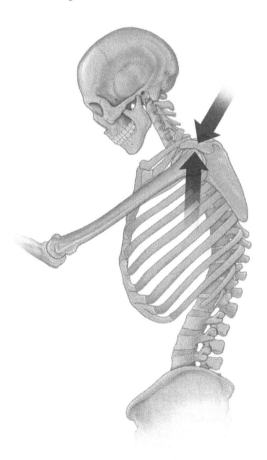

Figure 10.3 Posture's effect on the shoulder joint

As we've discovered in different ways throughout this book, daily habits can create muscular restriction that inhibits the fullest range of motion. It is useful to note that a slumped posture in the torso not only affects the spine but also the movement of the shoulder joint. When we crane forward to see a computer screen or read signs while driving, forward head posture creates compression in the shoulder joint. Take a moment to visualize the balance of the head at the AO joint and reconsider length through the spine. Now the integrity of the arm structure is available for efficient action. The chest, thoracic spine, and shoulder girdle naturally readjust to promote freedom of movement.

Exploration: Actions of the Glenohumeral Joint

Stand in a comfortable position with weight in both feet or sit at the edge of a chair so your arms can swing freely with the elbows extended. Begin with a mental practice to organize dynamic alignment through anatomical visualizations. Envision the tripod of balance in both feet and the poise of the head at the top of the spine. Move your glenohumeral joint through the following actions.

1. Flexion: Think of the thumbs leading the action and swing the arm forward. Can you swing the arms without letting the head and neck move forward?
2. Extension: Swing the arm directly behind you. How does your spine react to this action?
3. Abduction: Bring both arms out to the side up to shoulder height. Note your spine and ribcage response to this action.
4. Adduction: Let the arms move back down and cross in front of the body, so your wrists cross. Note your spine and ribcage response to this action.
5. Medial rotation: Rotate the whole arm inward from the shoulder joint. Bring attention to the alignment of your head and neck.
6. Lateral rotation: Rotate the whole arm outward from the shoulder joint. Bring attention to the alignment of your head and neck.
7. Circumduction: Move the arm in a large circle, swinging front, overhead, and back behind you to complete the circle. Can you find integrity in this action without involving the spine?

The glenohumeral actions work in collaboration with the movement of the scapula (shoulder blade). This relationship is called the scapulohumeral rhythm. When the scapulohumeral rhythm is well coordinated, the arms work efficiently.

Exploration: The Motions of the Scapula

You can perform this exploration on your own or with a partner. If using pairs, Partner A stands in front of Partner B with both partners facing the same direction. Partner B places their hands on the scapulae of Partner A. This placement will provide a tactile sensory experience for both partners of the gliding movement that the scapula performs in order to support arm and shoulder movement. If in pairs, Partner A moves through the following steps.

1. Elevation: Lift the shoulder blades toward your ears.
2. Depression: Press the shoulder blades back down along the ribs.
3. Adduction (retraction): Hug your shoulder blades together in toward the spine.
4. Abduction (protraction): Move the shoulder blades away from the spine.
5. Upward rotation: The natural swing of the inferior tip of the scapula is to swing away from the spine and upward. Start with your arms down by your sides. Move the arms out in front of you and then overhead; sense the motion of the inferior scapula gliding slightly up and out as indicated in Figure 10.4.
6. Downward rotation: The inferior tip of the scapula swings down and toward the spine. This action can be sensed as you return your arms by your side.

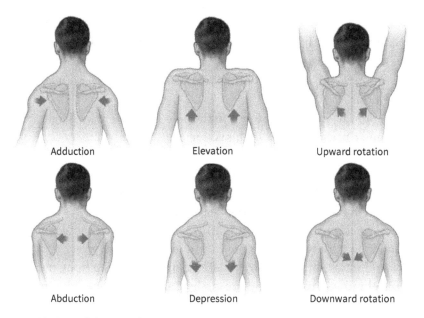

Adduction	Elevation	Upward rotation
Abduction	Depression	Downward rotation

Figure 10.4 Motions of the scapula

Exploration: Myth of Securing the Scapulae

1. Hold your shoulder blades down and squeeze them together behind you to broaden your chest. This action is depression and protraction of the scapulae.
2. Maintain this position as you attempt to move your arms through familiar movements from your dance classes.
3. Pause and release the holding.

4. Now permit the scapulae to glide in response to the action of the arms as you move through the movements once again.

Your Findings and Why They Matter

The scapula is like a leaf on a stream. It glides and moves in response to the actions of the spine, shoulder, and breath. It is not fixed. It can restrict motion if we think we must force the shoulder blades down the back and secure the scapula with tension. Overcontraction of a muscle group prevents the organic scapulohumeral rhythm and can impede expressivity in the arms (Figure 10.5).

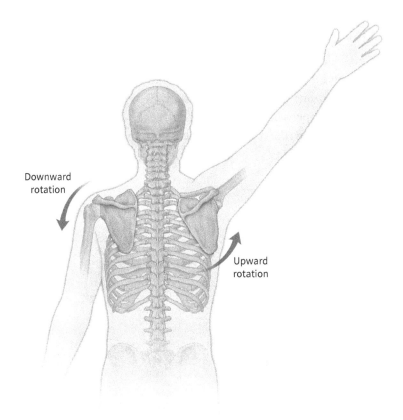

Figure 10.5 Scapulohumeral rhythm

The Anatomy: Muscular Support for Arms

The primary muscles supporting all the actions of the glenohumeral joint are the four muscles of the rotator cuff: supraspinatus, infraspinatus, teres minor, and subscapularis (Figure 10.6). Each of these muscles connects the glenohumeral ball-and-socket joint to the rest of the torso and supports its full range of action.

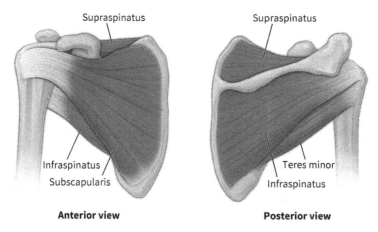

Supraspinatus

Supraspinatus

Infraspinatus
Subscapularis

Teres minor
Infraspinatus

Anterior view

Posterior view

Figure 10.6 Muscles of the rotator cuff

The latissimus dorsi and trapezius muscles on the posterior torso and the pectoralis major on the front are large superficial muscles that stabilize the shoulder and trunk. The latissimus spans the broad swath of the back, then spirals to insert onto the front of the upper arm at the upper third of the bicipital ridge (Figure 10.7). The pectoralis major spans the front of the chest from the sternum to the upper third of the bicipital ridge on the humerus (Figure 10.8).

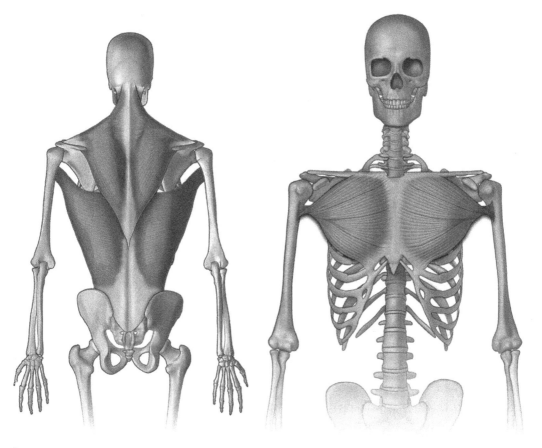

Figure 10.7 Latissimus dorsi and trapezius

Figure 10.8 Pectoralis major

Envision the latissimus muscle originating at the sacrum, fanning out, and spiraling around to insert to the front of your upper arms. It, along with the pectoralis major, is like the broad mainsail of a ship supporting you when you want to navigate the arms for expression.

Mindfulness in Dance Class

Do you ever notice your shoulders lifting unintentionally while you are dancing? In the moments before you begin a movement exercise, you can use that time to practice the 4Rs. Recognize what is happening. Release unnecessary tension. Recruit a new choice to let go of tensing the shoulders as a way to Restore the body during action. You can consider the tripod of balance at the feet, the balance at the AO joint, and the muscular support of the latissimus dorsi and pectoralis major.

Learning the balanced support of the superficial latissimus dorsi and pectoralis major to sustain expressive use of the arm structure is a two-part process of (1) opening through your front without shearing the ribs forward, and (2) supporting through the back without pinching the shoulder blades in and down. Let the shoulder blade glide into action easily with deep central support and see how this affects your dancing.

Mindfulness in Daily Life

Notice your overall posture when sitting at the computer or in class. For example, if you are in a C-curve, you may feel the glenohumeral joint rolled forward. Is the scapula in elevation or protraction? Decide whether this is a useful position for what you are doing. Is it a habit or is it a choice? Notice your arm placement while sleeping. Does your sleep position support a balanced arm structure? Try using different comfortable alternatives.

The Anatomy: Skeletal Features and Alignment of the Hand and Forearm

The elbow forms a hinge where the humerus and the ulna connect. Like all hinge joints, the elbow specifically allows flexion and extension. The forearm has two bones: the radius and the ulna (Figure 10.9). The movement in forearm rotation occurs at the radioulnar joint.

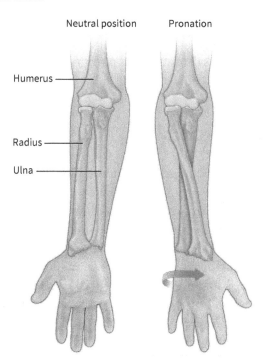

Neutral position   Pronation

Humerus

Radius

Ulna

Figure 10.9 Bones of the forearm

Exploration: Pronation and Supination

1. Begin with your arms by your side.
2. Bend at the elbows and hold your palms facing up; this is supination.
3. Turn your palms down; this is pronation.
4. Try both actions again and bring mindfulness to moving only from the elbows.

The actions of supination and pronation do not involve the shoulder girdle; therefore, movement is not required in the neck, shoulders, or upper arm. Often, we inadvertently hunch the shoulders into elevation and protraction when moving the forearms to a face-down position (pronation). The image demonstrates the action of the radius as it rotates around the ulna.

It is crucial to consider the alignment of the hand, wrist, and forearm in relation to the upper arm when load bearing, similar to being mindful of the alignment of the foot, knee, and hip when landing from a jump. The distal head of the radius on the thumb side of your wrist is more prominent and thicker than the distal head of the ulna. Because the distal head of the radius is thicker, it is better suited to weight-bearing. Therefore, during weight-bearing, it is more supportive for the whole arm structure to press the weight of the hands toward the index finger and thumb to distribute the weight through the hand and wrist.

Exploration: Loadbearing through the Arm Structure

1. Arrive in a tabletop position on all fours. Align your shoulders over your wrists, and your hips over your knees.
2. Establish your foundation. Let the thumbs be shoulder distance apart and the knees hip-width apart. Create space between your fingers and lengthen them away from your wrist. Allow your middle finger to point forward. Press the weight of your hands more toward the index finger and thumb for the most skeletal support.
3. With this foundation through your palms, encourage the inside of your elbow (antecubital fossa) to face toward your thumb. Imagine the full width of your collarbones (clavicles) from your sternoclavicular joint to your acromioclavicular joint. Allow the head of your humerus to nestle comfortably in the glenoid fossa of the scapula (the shoulder joint socket). Maintain this alignment in your arms as you tuck your toes under and straighten your legs for a plank pose.

Mindfulness in Daily Life

When you are sitting at your computer or chopping vegetables, notice how the action of the axial skeleton impacts the motion available to you in your appendicular skeleton. Is your thoracic spine in flexion, creating an impingement in the shoulder? Are you utilizing the glenohumeral joint and scapula to aid in the action of pronation or supination of the elbow when it is unnecessary? It is critical to differentiate the actions of the glenohumeral joint, the actions of the scapula, and the actions of the elbow and wrist. By moving efficiently within the structures of the arm, dancers can discover full range of motion at each joint and embody the expressivity required by the aesthetic they are performing.

Exploration: Snow Angel to Release Arm Tension

This activity has the nickname of the snow angel because it feels like a slower, mindful version of that activity we perform when falling on our backs in the snow to make an imprint of an angel in new-fallen snow. You can perform the snow angel standing along a wall or lying down on the floor. Read through the instructions and then explore the actions at a slow, reflective pace.

1. Begin on the floor in a semi-supine position or standing along a wall. Rest with elbows extended, palms resting approximately six to eight inches from your side body, and palms facing up.
2. With the palms facing up, move both arms away from your hips toward your head (abduction). Move about 2 or 3 inches and rest.
3. Flip the hands to face down, slowly leading with the fingertips, sensing the rotation at the radius and ulna of the forearm.
4. Turn the palms to face up again by initiating the action through the fingertips and move the hands upward a few more inches up and out to the side. Then flip the hands to face down and rest.
5. Flip the palms to face up again and move the arms to or above shoulder height. Pause here and allow for a few cycles of breath.
6. Reverse the process to return the arms down by your sides. When moving the arms back down, the palms continue to flip (pronation and supination) during the descent.
7. Pause and rest to allow for a moment to release any tension.

Your Findings and Why They Matter

The exploration engages the four muscles of the rotator cuff and the muscles of the forearm to release unnecessary tension. An effective warm-up before class is to open the arm structure and release tension to enhance the expressivity of the arms during class. It is also a wonderful reset for the arm structure at the end of a day.

Mindfulness in Dance Class and Daily Life

Think of an arm action performed during warm-up in dance class. Try it in your usual approach to this movement. Next, try it by leading with the fingertips. Note whether the body feels differently when performing the movement through distal initiation.

When reaching for something on a shelf, such as a coffee mug, or raising an arm to ask a question, notice where you like to initiate this movement. Play with different approaches to the same action of the arms. Initiate it distally from your fingertips. Initiate it more proximally from your shoulders. Explore the differences.

11

Breath

Breathing is a fundamental muscular action that affects all dance expression. We breathe automatically and unconsciously while moving through daily tasks. Breath can also be accessed in intricate ways through conscious control of the inhale and exhale. The respiratory mechanism supports neuromuscular stamina and cardiovascular health. In dance, the use of conscious breath can support artistic phrasing and expressivity. It is as important to deepen our understanding of the breathing mechanism as it is to understand the function of hips, knees, and ankles. Breathing practices provide opportunities to improve respiratory function, reduce excess tension and stress, and improve expressivity in movement.

Exploration: An Investigation of Breathing Patterns

1. Bring attention to your breath. Visualize where you see your breath going as it comes into the body during inhalation and its journey through to exhalation.
2. Note the length of your inhalations and exhalations. You might use a counting system to give yourself a way to measure the duration of your breath.
3. Take time to explore each of the following manners of breathing. Inhale through your nose and exhale out your mouth. Inhale through your mouth and exhale out your nose. Inhale and exhale through the nose. Inhale and exhale through the mouth. Notice how you prefer to breathe.

We develop movement habits for breath just as we have patterns for standing, walking, and sitting. The unconscious, easeful breathing that occurs during daily living is called tidal breath—allowing the breath to come in and out like the tides of the ocean. The moment you bring attention to it, however, your breath shifts out of this unconscious rhythm. Therefore, the duration of inhalation and exhalation you noted is not your tidal breathing pattern, but it may be an indication of how you habitually breathe.

The Anatomy: The Thoracic Cage

The lungs are housed in a skeletal structure known as the thoracic cage—commonly referred to as the rib cage. This cage comprises 12 pairs of ribs, the sternum or breastbone on the anterior side and the twelve thoracic vertebrae on the posterior side.

Functional Awareness. Second Edition. Nancy Romita and Allegra Romita, Oxford University Press.
© Oxford University Press 2023. DOI: 10.1093/oso/9780197586815.003.0012

This area houses the esophagus, the heart, and the lungs. There are 7 true ribs (1 to 7) on each side that attach directly to the sternum. Ribs 8 through 11 insert onto costal cartilage and rib 12 is a floating rib (Figure 11.1). The anterior portion of the ribs have greater expansion because of the costal cartilage in the front of the body.

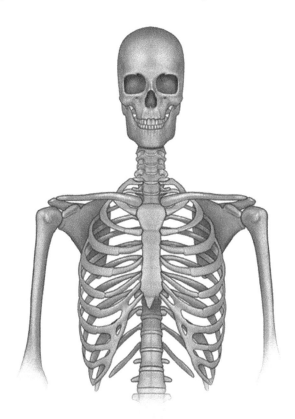

Figure 11.1 The thoracic cage

Exploration: Sensing the Lungs and Diaphragm

1. Visualize the thoracic cage and where your lungs are in your own torso. How high up do the lungs go? How far down into the torso do the lungs extend? Remember how you've mapped your lungs for future reference.

The Anatomy: The Location of the Lungs

The knowledge of the anatomical placement of the lungs and an understanding of the movement function of breathing can help reveal your unconscious or potentially ineffective breathing patterns. Many people have an inaccurate body map of the lungs. An unconscious mis-map of the lungs and misconception about breathing can lead to idiosyncratic breathing patterns that inhibit full cardiovascular capacity. Inefficient breathing patterns also have an effect on musicality and expressivity in dance. While examining Figure 11.1, note that the lungs begin at the first rib, just above the collarbone or clavicle, and inferiorly rest between the fourth and fifth rib. There is no lung tissue below the fifth rib. One cue sometimes used to help students breathe is "breathe into your belly." This anatomically inaccurate suggestion, although a metaphor that can encourage muscular support for breathing, also leads to misunderstanding the location of the lungs.

Take note of the composition of the lungs. The left lung is smaller than the right to accommodate the presence of the heart on the left side of the body. The lungs are composed of pathways for the air to travel called bronchial tubes. The air then moves to 480 million (on average) tiny sacs called alveoli (Ochs et al., 2004). The alveoli serve a very important function: they allow the lungs and the blood to exchange oxygen and carbon dioxide when you inhale or exhale, which is an essential act of living. Examine the lungs in Figure 11.2 and note the bronchial tubes and the tiny sacs at the ends. This physiological system exchanges the carbon dioxide and oxygen. Take a breath and imagine the air traveling along the pathways to the sacs and think of filling the alveoli as you are breathing in. Visualize the air being expelled from the lungs via those same pathways as you exhale.

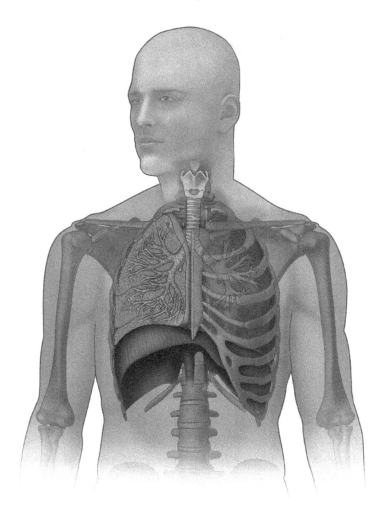

Figure 11.2 The lungs and the diaphragm

The Anatomy: Muscular Support for Breath

Diaphragmatic Breathing

The diaphragm is primarily responsible for the action of breathing. This large muscle covers the full circumference of the rib cage. The diaphragm expands and contracts the lower ribs to generate the lungs' intake of oxygen and expulsion of carbon dioxide. The diaphragm has two sets of fibers that look a bit like a tail, called the crus or crura. The crus interdigitates with the fibers of a muscle called the psoas. The psoas contributes to deep postural support and hip flexion, and it functions with the diaphragm during the action of breathing (Sajko & Stuber, 2009). The transverse abdominis also interdigitates with the inferior portion of the diaphragm. These deep muscles of abdominal and core support are inextricably linked to breathing (Figure 11.3).

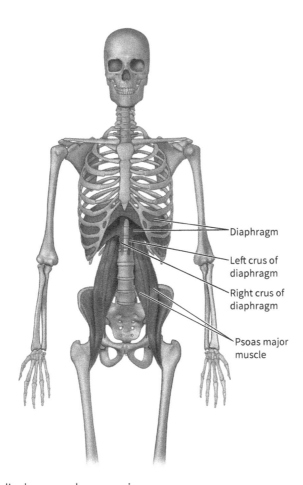

Figure 11.3 The diaphragm and psoas major

Exploration: The Diaphragm/Psoas Connection

1. Stand with the pelvis in anterior tilt and lock your knees.
2. Try to take a deep breath in.
3. Now soften the knees, release the anterior pelvic tilt, and find a neutral pelvic position.
4. Take several breaths in this standing position.

When the pelvis is in anterior tilt, the psoas can restrict full diaphragmatic action. You might notice quite a difference in the ability to take in air. With knees and back tight, the psoas cannot permit the diaphragm to easefully expand and contract, reducing breathing capacity.

Intercostal Breathing

Intercostal breathing or thoracic breath utilizes the intercostal muscles as the primary initiator for the action of breath. The intercostal muscles rest in between the ribs and help expand them to create space in the chest cavity to elicit breath. The intercostal muscles naturally engage actively in the action of breathing when the psoas major and transversus abdominis are being used to stabilize the lower back.

Exploration: Sequential Expansion of Intercostal Breath

1. Sit upright without using the back of the chair for support. Gently engage the core abdominals to stabilize the pelvis.
2. Place your hands on the sides of the ribs and inhale while sensing how the intercostal muscles expand the rib cage.
3. Inhale for a count of 3. Hold the breath for 3 counts, and then exhale 1, 2, 3.
4. Inhale for a count of 4. Hold the breath for 4 counts, and then exhale 1, 2, 3, 4.
5. Inhale for a count of 5. Hold the breath for 5 counts, and then exhale 1, 2, 3, 4, 5.
6. Return to tidal breathing and reflect on this process.

Sequential expansion of the intercostals through controlled breathing can enhance cardiovascular health, which enables dancers to perform through rigorous demands in classwork and performance. There is potential to stretch and strengthen these small muscles between the ribs. A dance educator and colleague of ours was once a synchronized swimmer. She was deeply practiced in progressive breath holding during her group's swimming routines. While she was training as a swimmer, she was also dancing. A dance costume designer was taking measurements and measured her ribcage circumference as 36 inches. When she stopped synchronized swimming and was no longer practicing progressive breath-holding techniques, her chest measurement reduced two whole inches! Practicing controlled breathing methods can help develop resilience in the muscles activating the breathing mechanism and encourage health in respiratory function as well as enhance expressivity in movement.

Auxiliary Respiratory Breathing

The auxiliary respiratory system accesses breath capacity in the upper lungs, including the lung tissue above the first rib. To access the upper third of the lungs, the scalene muscles of the neck lift the ribs to aid in breathing. The scalenes are a group of muscles originating on the front or anterior portion of the neck and cervical vertebrae and insert at the first rib and second rib (Figure 11.4). This attachment of the scalenes at the ribs provides a pull on the upper third of the thoracic cage to create space for respiration, expanding the upper portion of the ribs and allowing the upper lungs to fill.

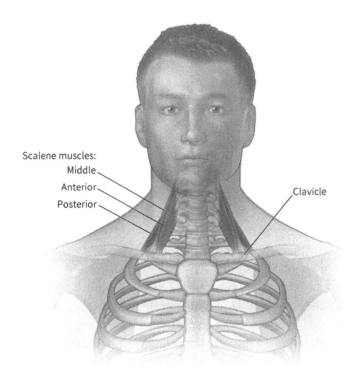

Figure 11.4 The scalene muscles

Exploration: Connecting to Auxiliary Respiratory Breath

1. Lift the head and chest into spinal extension.
2. Notice your breath in response to this action. Did you hold your breath? Some dancers hold their breath while embodying extension through the cervical and thoracic spine. The lack of breath can sometimes cause a brief dizziness or "seeing stars."
3. Try the action again with a breath into the upper third of your lungs as you extend back. Allow the muscles of your neck to support you as well. To bring the spine upright, release the head with a slight nod of the chin as you exhale to return. Sense how purposeful breath can support this motion.

How does this feel? Did you notice a difference when you were supported by breath? Is this similar to or different from your habit for breath during a back bend? In daily life, people with a habit of speaking and taking breaths through the mouth also activate the muscles in the upper third of the rib cage and the scalene muscles. This pattern, whether conscious or unconscious, can create unnecessary tension in the neck if it is the primary breathing pattern.

Exploration: Breathing Meditation

The following movement exploration offers an opportunity to enhance breath potential through the three types of breathing: diaphragmatic breath, intercostal breath, and auxiliary respiratory breath.

Part 1: Making Space for Breath

1. Place your hands at your lower abdomen. Sense the movement in the lower part of your torso as you breathe. There is no need to force anything to happen. Notice whether there is movement under your hands or in the lower abdomen. This is diaphragmatic breathing.
2. Place your hands on your upper ribs. You can do this by crossing your arms across your chest so each hand lands on the opposite side of the rib cage, or in any way that feels accessible to you. Inhale through your nose and allow for a long exhalation out of your mouth. Notice whether there is movement in the region of the ribs underneath your palms. Sense the movement of the

intercostal muscles moving into three-dimensional expansion on the inhalation and releasing from expansion on the exhalation.

3. Place your hands on your upper chest near your collarbones and breathe into the upper lungs or auxiliary respiratory system. Notice whether there is any movement in the cervical spine as you inhale and exhale.

Part 2: Imagery as a Tool for Breathing

1. Think of the spine as a stainless-steel rod from between your ears down to your tailbone. Allow for breath while considering this image.
2. Shift the image to envisioning the spine as a soft weeping willow branch and the breath like the wind.
3. Visualize the spine as seaweed and notice how this shifts your breath.
4. Record your findings.

Mindfulness in Dance Class

Sometimes unconscious breathing habits can prevent full expression in dance. How does awareness of your breathing patterns affect musicality and expressivity? Explore this in a class by performing a phrase without thinking of your breath first. Then return to the same movement vocabulary with breath purposely choreographed into the phrase.

Mindfulness in Daily Life

Before you sleep, practice the three cycles of breathing to allow for a mindful exploration of the breathing systems. Notice your preference for breathing when you are tired, happy, sad, or excited. Observe the changes in how you are holding your body in relation to breath. If you change your breathing, does this change your body or your mood at all?

Your Findings and Why They Matter

Awareness leads to choice and choice leads to possibility! Becoming aware of your habits allows you to make purposeful choices when breathing. We are not advocating a particular type of breath. Each of the four types of breath (tidal, diaphragmatic, intercostal, and auxiliary) explored in this chapter can be useful, depending on the context or the intention of the movement. Invite yourself to recognize what is, release any unnecessary tension, and recruit a new way of being through anatomical visualization, in order to restore a sense of balance in breath.

12

Restore toward Balance

Rest and restorative practices are often overlooked, yet they are an important factor in conditioning the body and mind to attain one's fullest potential in dance. Rest practices are essential to general health, shaping physical skill development, cognitive performance, and emotional well-being (Watson, 2017). Ignoring restorative processes adversely affects physical and mental activities, which in turn decreases competency and consistency when performing motor skills (Charest, 2020). A lack of mindfulness toward recuperation is a recipe for potential injury. Rest calibrates the body's energy and improves the ability to sustain the physical rigor required in dance training and performance.

The practice of recuperation does not always mean to sleep or to stop all activity and do nothing. Active recovery is important as well. There are many approaches to active rest and restoration practice. Lulu Sweigaard coined the term Constructive Rest for the position of lying down in a semi-supine (on the back with the knees bent and feet flat on the floor) that promotes spinal alignment and the release of excess tension (Sweigard, 1974). There are many methods in somatic education (such as Alexander Technique, Bartenieff Fundamentals, Body Mind Centering, or Feldenkrais Method) that encourage rebalancing and restoring the body through exploring gentle restful movement. Functional Awareness is an approach for releasing unnecessary tension that uses anatomical visualizations and gentle body investigations to enhance understanding of movement function and heighten sensory awareness.

The practice of cooling down at the end of a dance class is one form of active recovery. Cooling down allows the same muscles that were fatigued during class to recover more effectively than if we were simply to stop moving. The relationship between exertion and recuperation is relative. Sitting and watching a movie can be restorative after taking a dance class, and sometimes going for a run can be restorative after sitting in front of a computer for many hours. Recuperation can also be active, depending on the prior task performed. If we go-go-go all the time, our bodies will fatigue in multiple ways. If we are completely sedentary, with the intention of resting, our bodies may fatigue in other ways. It is all about balance: discovering a balance of action and recovery throughout our day can be a useful way to move sustainably.

A primary obstacle is fatigue. Fatigue interferes with the process of balancing the body's rhythms of exertion and recuperation, and it compromises the potential for optimal performance; 90% of dance injuries are related to fatigue (Leiderbach, 2018). Fatigue is a general term that can refer to extreme exhaustion. This form of fatigue

Functional Awareness. Second Edition. Nancy Romita and Allegra Romita, Oxford University Press.
© Oxford University Press 2023. DOI: 10.1093/oso/9780197586815.003.0013

can be either acute (related to lifestyle rhythms or specific tasks) or chronic. We can experience this as cognitive overload (mental fatigue) or excessive performance of the motor system (physical fatigue). The term physical fatigue is also used within the context of muscle fatigue—referring to what happens when a specific muscle or muscle group is used to the point of decreasing the ability to produce power (Wan et al., 2017). Awareness of fatigue can help dancers develop strategies to improve overall well-being and resilience to reduce risk of injury.

Another significant form of fatigue is sleep deprivation. Sleep habits can support or compromise a healthy immune system. Sleep aids the body in restoring the micro tearing of muscle tissue that is a natural part of building a strong and resilient dancer. The body needs time to repair muscles, regain strength, and replenish energy through sleep. A regular sleep pattern is one key component for discovering a balance between exertion and recuperation. Dancers who display a regular sleep cycle of at least 8 full hours of rest are 68% less likely to be injured (Leiderbach, 2018). Organizing a schedule to support eight hours of sleep can definitely be challenging, yet this one factor has a significant impact on injury prevention and overall wellness.

The length of time we sleep is one aspect of sleep hygiene. Maintaining a consistent bedtime is another important aspect of sleep wellness. A regular sleep schedule enhances the ability to focus on a task for longer and reduces emotional distress (Young-Eun Noh, Morris, & Andersen, 2005). Think about it: the simple practice of going to sleep within the same 30-minute timeframe each night can both boost mental ability and reduce stress.

Exploration: 4RS and Sleep

1. **Recognize** your sleep pattern. Keep a sleep journal for one week and record what time you go to sleep, what time you rise in the morning, and how many hours of sleep you experience. Make a note of your general sense of being in the morning. Do you feel rested? At the end of the day reflect on your overall energy and mood.
2. **Release** unnecessary tension around your findings about sleep. Let go of assumptions or expectations. Make observations that will help you make positive choices based on your current sleep habits.
3. **Recruit** non-judgmental language to encourage shifts toward mindful sleep habits. Remind yourself that resting for eight hours supports dancing and whole health. Think about rest with the same rigor and discipline you use to think about dance training or teaching.
4. **Restore** the balance between activity and rest through practices in your daily life. Coax the body toward change so you can accept those shifts and begin to create adaptive patterns that better support the muscle rejuvenation that occurs during sleep. Our ability to sustain physical rigor relies on our ability to rest.

The important part is that you actually sleep. Take time to discover the process for sleep, rest, and active recovery that works for you, your body, and your current life rhythm. This may need to be redefined over time.

The Anatomy: Mental Practices to Improve Skill through Active Rest

Dance training is both cognitive and physical. Performing a complex dance phrase requires not just physical movement but mental focus and cognitive function as well. Mental fatigue during dance class or rehearsal can interfere with or prevent continued focus on a task (Charest, 2019). This may lead to the inability to perform a series of turns, jumps, or balance tasks successfully and consistently. A lapse in concentration or mental focus can also lead to injury. Mental practice outside of dance settings can improve skills and build and restore the body; it can be a form of active recovery. Mental practice offers an opportunity to rest the body while practicing steps and movements. Unlike sleep it is an active practice for the conscious brain that develops mental stamina for when you return to the studio. Mental practice can help improve your confidence in an action and improve your movement skill while in relative stillness.

Exploration: Releasing Unnecessary Tension

You may move through the following restorative explorations while sitting in a chair or lying down on your back with your knees bent in a semi-supine position.

Part 1: Right Side

1. Begin by lying down on the floor with your legs extended. Extend your arms by your side with the palms facing up. Let your body release into the floor. Yield to gravity. Allow the weight of your heels to sense the contact with the earth. Let the weight of your head be taken by the floor. Let your jaw release away from your upper teeth. Bring an easy attention to your breathing.

2. Notice your right leg from the hip to the tips of the toes. Contract the muscles in the right leg and hold on to this contraction. As you are contracting the right leg, notice your lower back. Did it also tense up? Consciously decide to release that unnecessary tension. Notice your shoulders. Are they tensing to help your leg contract? Think of letting go in the shoulders while continuing to tense the right leg.

3. Release the tension in the right leg now. Gently move the leg around in the hip socket and let go of the contraction.

4. Notice whether there is any difference between your just-contracted right leg and the other leg. Often there is a change in sensation between the two legs, demonstrating a shift in resting length in the muscle spindle that determines the level of tension needed for body action.

5. With your right arm, make a fist and tense the muscles of the entire arm from shoulder to fingers. Hold this pose. Notice your neck and see whether it is holding tension. Ask yourself to let your neck release. Notice whether your jaw has tightened, and if so, allow the lower jaw to release away from the upper teeth. Let your breathing support greater ease as you continue to contract the right arm.

6. Open the hand gently and release the tension in the arm. Move the arm in any easy pathway to help release the tension generated in the contraction.

7. Observe whether there is a difference between the right arm and the left. Do you sense any difference between the right and left sides of the body? Do you notice some parts of your body tense up even when asking a different region to engage? These unnecessary tensions deplete energy and contribute to inefficiency in action.

Part 2: Left Side

1. Notice your left leg from the hip to the tips of the toes. This time, before contracting the muscles in the left leg, ask yourself to pause and allow for a breath. Release unwanted tension from the extraneous body parts as you contract the muscles of the left leg. Hold the left leg firmly tense as you continue easy breathing, asking yourself to let go of unnecessary tension.

2. Release the contraction in the left leg now. Gently move the leg around a bit. Notice how both legs feel.

3. Before you make a fist and tense the muscles of the entire left arm, notice your neck and see whether it is holding tension. Ask yourself to let the neck release. Notice whether your jaw has tightened and if so, allow the lower jaw to release away from the upper teeth. Make a fist with the left hand and contract the muscles in the left arm. Can you sense that you are doing the required action with less overall tension in the body?

4. Open the hand gently and release the tension in the arm. Move the arm in an easy pathway to help release the tension.

5. Bring both shoulders up by your ears and hold them there. Continue to hold them up as you check in with your breathing. Ask yourself, "Where can I do less and still hold my shoulders up?" It is a playful exploration.

6. Now release both shoulders down and come to a place of ease in the whole body. Notice the general tension level in your body. Did this change from the beginning of the exploration?

Your Findings and Why They Matter

In practicing this body/brain game and inhibiting your habitual responses to do simple actions, the body teaches itself to let go of unwanted tension. When you contract, tense, and hold certain parts of the body for 5 to 10 seconds and then release this tension, it enables the muscles to shift the relaxed resting length of the muscle fibers. This exploration heightens your awareness of tension and invites the body to release unnecessary muscle contraction that is a source of body fatigue and stress.

Exploration: Balancing Hips, Knees, Feet

1. Begin in a semi-supine position. Take a moment to release into the floor. Yield to gravity. Notice your breathing, without judgment or expectation. Notice inspiration as the air spills in and ask yourself to consider letting go of unnecessary tension on the exhalation.
2. Consider the tripod of balance in both feet. Is your weight equally distributed through all three points?
3. Gently extend the right knee and slide the leg straight out along the floor. As you slide, be mindful of maintaining the tripod of balance. Maintain the leg in parallel even after it is completely straight.
4. Pause for a moment. Ask yourself if there are any places in your body where you can let go of any unnecessary tension.
5. Draw the leg into flexion by sliding the foot along the floor. As the leg moves from straight out to a bent knee position find the tripod of the foot on the floor. Notice if you favor the outside or inside of the foot through inversion or eversion during this process. As you rest the foot back onto the floor with the knee bent, be mindful of the tripod of balance and let all three points of contact have equal weight into the floor.
6. Repeat this pattern 3 times on the same leg. This allows for neural repatterning in the body.
7. Repeat this process with the other leg. Finish the sequence with both knees bent. Let yourself make small adjustments in the body to allow for length in the spine to support the shifts in the legs.

Your Findings and Why They Matter

This quiet restorative process invites awareness of habit, develops new patterning for bending and straightening the leg, and restores balance in the musculature of the legs. It is restful and a useful alternative to foam rolling as an approach to releasing thigh tension before or following dance class.

Mindfulness in Daily Life

Throughout your day, invite the body to restore toward balance by recognizing what your body is doing at the moment, releasing unnecessary muscular tension or judgment around what you noticed, and recruiting a new way of being (through an anatomical visualization and making a different movement choice). This active reflective practice of the 4Rs can be a form of recovery for your body and mind.

Beach Glass and Shells

Functional Awareness is embodied anatomy through reflective practice. This practice includes something that we call "beach glass and shells." When you've come to the end of a dance class, workshop, presentation, or book, imagine that experience as a long walk on the beach (Figure 12.1). On that walk, you've seen a lot. You've seen sand, water, umbrellas, people, seagulls, etc. Perhaps you've also seen a lovely shell or piece of smooth beach glass that you've chosen to pick up and take with you. Take a moment to consider the gems (or shells) that you've collected throughout your time reading this book. During your journey of reading the book, what discoveries or ideas engaged you? What questions or further inquiries bubbled up during the course of the chapters? What are those morsels of information or experiences that you've picked up along the way? Take time to reflect on what concepts, imagery, or movement explorations might be a piece of beach glass for you. Glance back through the book and find one thing in each chapter to record as your beach glass or shell. It can be something you question and wish to investigate further or it can be something that engaged you and you want to put into practice.

Figure 12.1 A long walk on the beach

Mindfulness Moving Forward

Continue to bring awareness to your habitual patterns of movement and how they affect your dancing and your everyday life. Continue to seek the end-ranges of movement and explore the reaches of your artistry. Enjoy the energetic satisfaction of exertion and also allow time for recuperation. Recuperation can be as simple as a moment's pause to recognize, release, recruit, and restore. We invite you to utilize Functional Awareness: Anatomy in Action and the shells and beach glass you've collected as tools for discovery, exploration, and change.

Glossary of Terms in Human Anatomy

Planes of the Body

transverse or horizontal: plane divides the body into upper and lower parts, superior and inferior.

median or mid-sagittal: plane divides the body in right and left halves.

coronal or frontal: plane divides the body into front and back, or anterior and posterior parts.

Anatomical Terms of Reference

anterior: indicates the front of the body.

posterior: indicates the back of the body.

superior: indicates a position on the body above the point of reference.

inferior: indicates a position on the body below the point of reference.

proximal: indicates closer to the trunk, or joint of reference.

distal: indicates farther from the trunk or joint of reference.

flexion: indicates movement in the sagittal plane that takes the body forward.

extension: indicates movement in the sagittal plane that takes the body backward.

ipsilateral: indicates movement on the same side of the body.

contralateral: indicates movement on opposite sides of the body.

abduction: indicates movement away from the median plane.

adduction: indicates movement toward the median plane.

medial rotation: indicates movement in the transverse (horizontal) plane moving inward.

lateral rotation: indicates movement in the transverse (horizontal) plane moving outward.

superficial: designates position on the exterior part of the body.

deep: designates a position on an internal part of the body.

supination: indicates movement with the palm of the hand facing forward/up.

pronation: indicates a movement with the palm of the hand facing backward/down.

axial skeleton: skull, hyoid bone, spine, sacrum, coccyx, thoracic cage.

appendicular skeleton: scapula, humerus, radius, ulna, carpals, metacarpals, phalanges, pelvis, femur, tibia, patella, fibula, tarsals, metatarsals, phalanges.

Works Cited

Castagnoli, C., Cecchi, F., Del Canto, A., Paperini, A., Boni, R., Pasquini, G., Vannetti, F., & Macchi, C. (2015). Effects in short and long term of global postural reeducation (GPR) on chronic low back pain: A controlled study with one-year follow-up. *The Scientific World Journal*, 271436. doi:10.1155/2015/271436

Charest, J., & Grandner, M. A. (2020). Sleep and athletic performance: Impacts on physical performance, mental performance, injury risk and recovery, and mental health. *Sleep Medicine Clinics*, 15(1), 41–57. doi: 10.1016/j.jsmc.2019.11.005

Conti, S., & Wong, Y. S. (2001). Foot and ankle injuries in the dancer. *Journal of Dance Medicine and Science*, 5(2), 43–50.

Dowd, I. (1990). *Taking root to fly: Articles on functional anatomy*. New York, NY: Irene Dowd.

H'Doubler, M. (1998). *Dance, a creative art experience*. Madison, WI: University of Wisconsin Press.

Leiderbach, M. (2008). Epidemiology of dance injuries: Biosocial considerations in the management of dancer health: Strategies for the prevention and care of injuries to dancers. *American Physical Therapy Association Orthopedic Section Monograph, Independent Study Course* 18, 1–3, La Crosse, Wisconsin.

Liederbach, M., Kremenic, I. J., Orishimo, K. F., Pappas, E., & Hagins, M. (2014). Comparison of landing biomechanics between male and female dancers and athletes, part 2: Influence of fatigue and implications for anterior cruciate ligament injury. *The American Journal of Sports Medicine*, 42(5), 1089–1095. doi: 10.1177/0363546514524525

Noh, Y., Morris, T., & Andersen, M. B. (2005). Psychosocial factors and ballet injuries. *International Journal of Sport and Exercise Psychology*, 3, 79–90.

Noll, M., Candotti, C. T., da Rosa, B. N., do Valle, M. B., Antoniolli, A., Vieira, A., & Loss, J. F. (2017). High prevalence of inadequate sitting and sleeping postures: A three-year prospective study of adolescents. *Scientific Reports*, 7(1), 14929. doi: 10.1038/s41598-017-15093-2

Ochs, M., et al. (2004). The number of alveoli in the human lung. *American Journal of Respiratory and Critical Care Medicine*, 169(1), 120–124. doi: 10.1164/rccm.200308-1107OC

Orishimo, K. F., Liederbach, M., Kremenic, I. J., Hagins, M., & Pappas, E. (2015). Kinematic sequencing differences between dancers and team-sport athletes during jumping and landing, 1612. *Medicine & Science in Sports & Exercise* 47(5S), 426. doi: 10.1249/01.mss.0000477601.95626.52

Orishimo, K. F., Liederbach, M., Kremenic, I. J., Hagin, M., & Pappas, E. (2014). Comparison of landing biomechanics between male and female dancers and athletes, part 1: Influence of sex on risk of anterior cruciate ligament injury. *The American Journal of Sports Medicine*, 45(5), 1082–1088.

Pallaro, P. (2007). *Authentic movement: Moving the body, moving the self, being moved: A collection of essays, Vol. II*. Philadelphia: Jessica Kingsley.

Sajko, S., & Stuber, K. (2009). Psoas major: A case report and review of its anatomy, biomechanics, and clinical applications. *The Journal of Canadian Chiropractic Organization*, 53(4), 311–318.

Slimani, M., Tod, D., Chaabene, H., Miarka, B., & Chamari, K. (2016). Effects of mental imagery on muscular strength in healthy and patient participants: A systematic review. *Journal of Sports Science & Medicine*, 15(3), 434–450.

Sweigard, L. (1974). *Human Movement Potential: Its Ideokinetic Facilitation*. New York, NY: Harper Row.

Todd, M. (1937). *The thinking body*. Brooklyn, NY: Dance Horizons.

Wan, J., Qin, Z., Wang, P., Sun, Y., & Liu, X. (2017). Muscle fatigue: General understanding and treatment. *Experimental & Molecular Medicine*, 49, e384. doi:10.1038/emm.2017.194

Watson, A. M. (2017). Sleep and athletic performance. *Current Sports Medicine Reports*, 16(6), 413–418. doi: 10.1249/JSR.0000000000000418

Index

For the benefit of digital users, indexed terms that span two pages (e.g., 52–53) may, on occasion, appear on only one of those pages.

Figures are indicated by *f* following the page number